POLICY AND PRACTICE IN HEALTH AND SOCIAL CARE
NUMBER SEVENTEEN

Residential Child Care

POLICY AND PRACTICE IN HEALTH AND SOCIAL CARE

See www.dunedinacademicpress.co.uk for details of all our publications

POLICY AND PRACTICE IN HEALTH AND SOCIAL CARE

SERIES EDITORS

JOYCE CAVAYE and ALISON PETCH

Residential Child Care: Between Home and Family

Graham Connelly

Research and Qualifying Courses Manager, CELCIS (Centre for Excellence for Looked After Children in Scotland), Senior lecturer, Glasgow School of Social Work, University of Strathclyde, Glasgow

and

Ian Milligan

International Lead, CELCIS (Centre for Excellence for Looked After Children in Scotland), Senior lecturer, Glasgow School of Social Work, University of Strathclyde, Glasgow

EDINBURGH ◆ LONDON

First published in 2012 by
Dunedin Academic Press Ltd

Head Office:
Hudson House, 8 Albany Street,
Edinburgh EH1 3QB

London Office:
The Towers, 54 Vartry Road,
London N15 6PU

ISBN 978–1-780460–00–0
© 2012 Graham Connelly and Ian Milligan

British Library Cataloguing in Publication Data
A catalogue record for this book is available from the British Library

Typeset by Makar Publishing Production
Printed by CPI Group (UK) Ltd., Croydon, CR0 4YY

Jon-Marc Creaney 1971–2011

This book is dedicated to the memory of the late
Jon-Marc Creaney, architect, who created wonderful designs for
children's houses, based on his empathic understanding of the
purpose of residential child care.

CONTENTS

SERIES EDITORS' INTRODUCTION

In Scotland around 1.5% of children under eighteen are looked after by the local authority. From this group, around 10% – more of the older age group, few of the very young – are placed in residential settings: children's homes, residential schools or secure care. For many, such settings have negative perceptions: they are regarded as a placement of 'last resort' for the most challenging, staffed by the less qualified. Yet it can be argued that this is exactly the group of young people for whom the provision should be of the highest standard.

In this volume Connelly and Milligan present a clear and engaging outline of the purpose and provision of residential care. They explain who is likely to be living in residential care, the policies that have driven its provision, and the daily practice in a residential setting. They highlight the tensions likely to emerge if the focus of residential provision is on temporary provision for an individual, when, for some, it may be more permanent and the group context will be an essential component. The concluding chapter explores in further detail the concept of social pedagogy, which is popular in the provision of residential care for children elsewhere in Europe, and the focus of some discussion in Scotland in recent years.

The argument for residential child care provided from the basis of a much more positive focus is exemplified in the consideration of design aspects of residential care. Rarely has this been a priority for quality provision, with the physical environment often dominated by considerations of security and risk reduction. Yet, as exemplified by one Scottish local authority, an ambition to provide surroundings that nurture and respect the young person should go hand in hand with policies that consider residential care as the optimum choice for a small number of young people at a particular stage in their life. The voices of young people, which are quoted throughout this volume, confirm why this is a critical area for both policy and practice.

Dr Joyce Cavaye
Faculty of Health and Social Care, The Open University in Scotland, Edinburgh

Professor Alison Petch
The Institute for Research and Innovation in Social Services (IRISS), Glasgow

ACKNOWLEDGEMENTS

The authors wish to acknowledge the particular assistance given to them in preparing this book by their colleague and friend Judy Furnivall. We would also like to thank our editor, Alison Petch, for her invaluable suggestions on an earlier draft. Others who have given their time freely to share their expertise are David Carver, Ben Farrugia, Sheila Gordon, Scott Hunter, Norma Lawrie, Caroline Richardson and Max Smart.

LIST OF ABBREVIATIONS

CAMHS	Child and Adolescent Mental Health Services
CCETSW	Central Council for Education and Training in Social Work
CEL	Chief Executive Letter (to health boards)
CELCIS	Centre for Excellence for Looked After Children in Scotland
CQSW	Certificate of Qualification in Social Work
CSS	Certificate in Social Service
DipSW	Diploma in Social Work
DOH	Department of Health
FAIR	Framework of Assessment and Intervention for Resilience
GIRFEC	Getting It Right For Every Child
HMI	Her Majesty's Inspectors of Schools
HMIE	Her Majesty's Inspectorate of Education
HMSO	Her Majesty's Stationery Office
HNC	Higher National Certificate
HSE	Health and Safety Executive
NISW	National Institute for Social Work
NRCCI	National Residential Child Care Initiative
PVG	Protection of Vulnerable Groups
SCRA	Scottish Children's Reporter Administration
SIRCC	Scottish Institute for Residential Child Care
SSSC	Scottish Social Services Council
SVQ	Scottish Vocational Qualification
SWIA	Social Work Inspection Agency
SWSI	Social Work Services Inspectorate
SWSIS	Social Work Services Inspectorate for Scotland
TCI	Therapeutic Crisis Intervention
TCRU	Thomas Coram Research Unit

UNCRC   United Nations Convention on the Rights of the Child
VOYPIC   Voice of Young People in Care

INTRODUCTION

The aim of this book is to provide an overview of residential child care in Scotland. It is not a practice manual and it does not attempt to give advice on direct work with children. It sets out to provide an account of the place of residential care for children 'looked after' by the state in contemporary Scotland. The book is written from the perspectives of the authors, both currently in academic posts, but both with considerable experience of direct contact with looked after children and care leavers. Its omissions and idiosyncrasies are our responsibility, but we acknowledge the influence of colleagues and young people who have willingly opened up to us about their experiences. *Residential Child Care: Between Home and Family* has no particular theoretical stance, but we hope that it has been influenced by two important values. One is the need to have high aspirations for children in public care, and the belief that those who have the privilege of influencing them deserve respect and encouragement. The second is the importance of hearing the voice of the looked after child. This is not to say that adults should always do what children want, but listening to children who are hurting is fundamental to the healing process.

Most children who are looked after by local authorities live in family-type settings, with either one or both parents, with other relatives or with foster carers. Despite the decline in the use of residential placements, group living settings continue to be important, positive care options, particularly for older children. Residential care epitomises public perceptions of the care system, and yet few members of the general population will have had direct experience of care settings. They may even express hostility to the presence of residential units near to where they live. Residential settings are most visible when things go wrong – absconding, damage to property, the abuse or even deaths of children while in care – and the consequences are reported by regulatory authorities and the media. In these circumstances the failings of workers will be graphically highlighted, but, with some notable exceptions, the everyday work of building relationships with children affected by the trauma that happens in families goes unrecognised. For the most part the work of care agencies is carried on out of sight. The sub-title of the book, *Between Home and Family*, signifies the importance of the residential setting as a therapeutic environment, providing more than mere accommodation, by offering children and adolescents skilled help to recover from trauma, and space to develop, while also acting as a relational bridge to their families.

The book is aimed mainly at students on social care, social work, teacher education, educational psychology and health-related courses, though we hope it will also be of interest to professionals working in children's services, to children's panel members, and professionals and volunteers in children's rights and advocacy services. We like to think that it will also appeal to the general reader, curious to know more about one aspect of the spectrum of care provision for children. Services for troubled children have been traditionally reluctant to describe their work for a general audience, for fear of provoking more opposition to their presence, and yet they do need to develop alliances in the communities where they are located. Indeed, many have been more open recently to showcasing their work, by having a presence on the web, by co-operating with journalists and even by agreeing to participate in reality television programmes. There is also a constant need for lay people to volunteer to be children's panel members, mentors and members of boards of management of children's charities.

The geographical context of the book is Scotland, though references are made, where appropriate, to policy and practice in other parts of the UK and in other countries. Scotland retained its unique legal system when it entered the Union with England and Wales in 1707, and as a consequence legislation governing family life and the welfare of children has always been particular to Scotland. Since the devolution of UK government in 1999 created a Scottish parliament and government assemblies in Northern Ireland and Wales, social policy throughout the UK has become more diverse and, some would argue, more interesting. While, inevitably, the authors have given more space to outlining the particular arrangements for looking after children in Scotland, the issues explored – the aim and function of residential care and the educational and health outcomes of care leavers – have application internationally.

Residential Child Care: Between Home and Family has seven chapters, each structured in a similar way, with an introduction, section headings and a summary of the key messages. Each chapter ends with a *Thinking outside the box* section, an invitation to the reader to engage in reflection, further reading or web-browsing by responding to questions posed by the authors. The structure of the book is as follows.

Chapter 1, Residential Care: A Home Away From Home, introduces residential care in both historical and contemporary contexts and distinguishes it from other forms of care for children looked after by local authorities and their partners.

In *Chapter 2, Residential Care: The Physical Environment,* we describe the physical environment of a modern residential child care setting. In particular, we consider ideas about what makes a place a 'home', and how reflections on ways in which children can be offered an experience that is 'family-like' have influenced aspects of design and location.

Chapter 3, Children's Stories and Children's Views, aims to help the reader understand the role of residential care in providing a home to children and young people. In it we outline different ways in which children's views about their experiences of living in residential care are gathered and articulated, principally on their behalf by advocacy and campaigning organisations, but also by service users themselves, and we also consider the extent to which these views are represented in research and policy development.

In *Chapter 4, Residential Care and Social Policy,* we examine the broader social policy context within which residential care is provided in Scotland. The chapter reviews how decisions about placing children are made and how these have been influenced by trends or 'fashions' in responding to the needs of children who come into contact with the justice and child welfare systems. Current trends in Scotland are considered in the light of practice in other countries. The chapter also looks at the concept of 'corporate parent' and the policy landscape which governs this idea.

Chapter 5, The Purpose and Function of Residential Child Care, is concerned with the important notion of what a residential placement can provide for children and young people, and the place of residential homes and schools in the spectrum of social services. We raise questions about aspirations in policy for a range of care options and the impact on provision of the generally acknowledged preference for family placement.

In *Chapter 6, Daily Residential Practice in a Risk-Averse Environment*, we consider how workers provide care in non-institutional forms while at the same time meeting the demands of a range of stakeholders, including the Care Inspectorate. We acknowledge that the task of providing non-institutional care, or 'homely care', is made more complex by factors external to the child care system.

Chapter 7, Group Care for Children and the Emergence of Social Pedagogy, concludes the book with the proposition that the *group* aspect of residential care has often been neglected, both in theory and practice. The chapter introduces the approach to residential work known as social pedagogy, which, while common in parts of Europe, has only relatively recently begun to make an impact in Scotland. We suggest that social pedagogy can build on the best-quality residential care in Scotland and provide a sound framework for training residential workers.

Summary

This introduction has explained that the aim of the book is to provide an overview of residential child care in the Scottish context, though the broader themes discussed are relevant to group care work in many countries.

Whether you are approaching the book as a student, an experienced practitioner, a volunteer or as an interested observer, we hope that you find the following seven chapters leave you better informed about residential care for looked after children and feeling better placed to ask questions about its contribution to services for children.

CHAPTER 1

Residential Care:
A Home Away From Home

Introduction

In this chapter we explain what residential care is and distinguish it from other forms of care for children looked after by the state. We outline the social and legal context within which residential care settings operate, and consider both the relationship between residential care and birth families and the changing use of residential care within social services provision. Finally, we discuss the role and training of residential child care staff.

What is residential care?

It is relatively uncommon for a child growing up in Scotland to live in a group setting. This experience is familiar to only two groups of children. The first group comprises the relatively small number of children who attend boarding schools for reasons of preference, family tradition or whose parents work abroad. There are also some children who live in school hostels during the week and travel home at weekends; these are mostly children from island communities or those who attend one of Scotland's six national centres of excellence, such as the Dance School of Scotland in Glasgow. The second group consists of children for whom the state provides residential care. Though these two groups of children may have experiences in common – such as living apart from their families – there are two clear ways in which they differ. In the first place, there are economic differences, since being in the care of the state is closely connected with social disadvantage and low family income. Secondly, while going to a boarding school is usually a positive choice – or at least parents intend it to be – and although some children, or their families, request that they should be taken into care, usually care placements are not a matter of choice, but rather result from compulsory measures made by a children's hearing or court.

Compulsory measures of 'supervision' are defined by the Children (Scotland) Act 1995[1] as actions taken for the 'protection, guidance, treatment or control' of children under a set of conditions (e.g. lack of parental care, failure to attend school regularly, committing an offence) specified in Section 52 (2) of the Act. In Scotland in 2011, more than 16,000 children were in the care of the state (Scottish Government, 2012b).[2] This figure accounted for 1.5% of all children up to age eighteen across the country, although the proportions of children in state care are higher in the larger cities (e.g. 2.8% in Glasgow). The Children (Scotland) Act 1995 refers to children in care as being 'looked after' by local authorities, a term that was introduced by the earlier Children Act 1989 in England and Wales. The term 'looked after' is used throughout the UK and in some other countries such as Australia. It was introduced to reduce the stigma associated with the term 'in care', but it has proved to be confusing, particularly in educational contexts. There are stories, hopefully apocryphal, of schools inflating the count of looked after children in official returns as a result of including children thought to be 'well looked after'. The central body that administers applications for most undergraduate courses in universities, UCAS, has included a voluntary declaration of looked after background within the application process since 2008, but the data collected have never been published because of concerns about their accuracy (personal communication). Discrepancies are found between social work and education statistical returns. Explanations include the possibility that schools either undercount children legally looked after because of ineffective communication with social work colleagues, or overcount them as a result of a failure to update records when a child ceases to be looked after.

The process of becoming looked after usually involves the child participating in a children's hearing, at which a panel of three volunteer members of the community considers background reports and listens to the views of the child, family members and professionals. If the panel concludes that compulsory measures of care are necessary it will specify whether these should be provided 'at home', i.e. with the child remaining in the usual family home (just over a third of all looked after children) or 'away from home'.

Some children are also admitted to residential or foster care through the voluntary agreement of the parents following a crisis or problem that has led to the involvement of a social worker. Children placed in this way come under Section 25 of the Children (Scotland) Act 1995. These children can remain in care for a long period, and parents retain their right to take their children home. If the difficulties that led to a child being admitted to care by voluntary agreement persist social workers may seek to have care transferred to 'compulsory measures' within the children's hearings' system.

Around half of all children looked after away from home live in family-type settings, either with trained foster carers or potential adoptive parents, or in so-called 'kinship' settings where a member of the close or extended family is officially recognised as the main carer. A minority (about 10%) of looked after children is cared for in group settings, including residential homes in the community (also called units, young people's centres or children's houses), residential schools and secure care settings. This figure is an average, however, and official statistics show that foster care is more common as a placement for younger children and residential care for older children. For example, 20% of 12–15-year-old, looked after children live in residential settings, compared with less than 3% of 5–11 year olds and a negligible proportion of under-fives.

The overall proportion of looked after children cared for in group settings has been falling for several years in comparison with increasing proportions of children living in foster and kinship placements. For example, in 1976, while 36% of looked after children lived in residential settings, 22% were in foster care. This decline in the relative importance of residential placements is mirrored by practice evident in the other constituent countries of the UK, and, while it is part of a common trend among developed countries, there are exceptions such as Denmark where 41% of looked after children live in residential care (Jackson and Cameron, 2010).

Despite the fall in the number of children living in residential settings in Scotland, their importance to the community has not declined, for three reasons. First, these facilities look after our most troubled, abused and neglected children. Second, the financial cost is considerable as local authorities spend about £250 million annually on placements, and while the number of children in residential placements remained stable between 2001–2 and 2008–9, expenditure increased by around 68% (Audit Scotland, 2010). Third, as we discuss later, the number of providers offering services has increased significantly.

The fall in the number of children looked after in residential settings can be explained by the prevalence of social work discourses, which have preferred family-type care settings over those provided in 'institutions' (Smith, 2009). It is important to be aware of the use of the term 'institution', which is nearly always applied in a pejorative fashion. Contemporary children's homes are small in scale precisely to avoid the inadequacies of large-group institutional care, but sometimes they are still described as such by those who are not in sympathy with any form of 'non-family' care. This shift in preference, which some might even describe as a change in fashion, may have unintended consequences. Smith argues that this policy change means that residential care has to 'pick up the pieces' when foster care placements break down and that there is 'a residualisation of residential child care, whereby only the most difficult to place young people are admitted' (Smith, 2009, p. 54).

There is a certain irony in the observation that as family structure has become more differentiated – and many children grow up in lone-parent households, 'blended' families with step-siblings or move between the homes of separated parents – group care settings provided by the state have become less common. It is a short step from being uncommon to being regarded as second best or the last resort. There are various reasons for the negative perceptions which have attached to residential child care. One, undoubtedly, is the wide publicity given to cases of the abuse or neglect of children in residential settings. Another, identified twenty years ago by the Skinner report, is the feeling among residential staff 'that the purpose of their work, and their contribution, are not sufficiently understood or valued' (Skinner, 1992). The National Residential Child Care Initiative (NRCCI), which reported to Scottish ministers in 2009, suggested that ambivalence towards residential care persists: 'Governments have repeatedly asserted that residential child care can and should be a positive choice, yet primacy is often given to family placements' (Hill, 2009, p. 13).

Contemporary residential child care does not pretend that it is a 'family', and full recognition is always given to a child's heritage and birth family, yet care is intended to be family-like in the sense that it aims to provide children with a secure, nurturing and stimulating environment where they experience warm, authentic care relationships with residential workers. Interestingly, some children report that their residential experience has been a family one, or 'it feels like a family' (Happer *et al.*, 2006, p. 11). For some children, residential care gives them an experience of 'normal' family life – doing ordinary things and receiving consistent care from adults – absent from a birth family life marked by extreme stress, dysfunction or abuse (Bolger and Miller, 2012).

Residential care settings

> The distinguishing feature of residential care compared with foster care is that children live with a group of other children looked after by paid staff who work on a shift basis and live elsewhere (Hill, 2009, p. 4).

The main providers of residential facilities for children are Scotland's thirty-two local authorities, the voluntary sector and independent providers (profit and non-profit making). Local authorities have traditionally been providers of children's homes, a legacy from the days before local government reorganisation in 1997 when there were fewer, larger authorities. There has, however, been a trend towards local authorities purchasing places in homes managed by independent providers. This practice was begun in order to meet the needs of smaller authorities, particularly for specialist placements (e.g. for children with additional support needs), but the extent of purchasing of placements has increased and consortia of local authorities are beginning to be established to share costs of commissioning services (ODS Consulting, 2011).

Residential schools and secure care facilities have traditionally been provided by the voluntary sector, with the Church of Scotland and the Catholic Church being the largest providers. Other significant providers include well-established local trusts, such as Kibble Education and Care Centre in Paisley and Balnacraig School in Perth. More recently, independent providers have opened schools, such as Troup House in Aberdeenshire and Spark of Genius in Paisley. A research exercise conducted by the Scottish Institute for Residential Child Care (SIRCC) and the Care Commission in March 2009 attempted to identify all the residential services in Scotland (Hill, 2009). This work established that thirty-one local authorities provided their own residential child care, while there was a total of fifty-nine voluntary, private and other independent organisations also offering services. The research found that the total number of providers had grown from seventy-two in 2004 to ninety in 2009.

Children's homes
Children's homes of the past were typically large houses, often the former residences of wealthy citizens which had seen many changes of function over the years. Their institutional status was signified on the exterior by a fire escape and by an office, meeting room and industrial kitchen inside. Whether located in a town or rural area, they were frequently far from the homes from which the resident children had been removed. Since the 1980s there has been a progressive trend towards smaller homes, and most now have fewer than ten children. Ninety percent of homes today provide for between two and nine children (Hill, 2009). The children's home estate in Scotland is now diverse: some older, larger properties remain; some providers have converted social housing; others have purchased family-sized properties on the domestic real-estate market. A more recent trend involves the use of planning regulations by local authorities to require private house developers to build a children's house within a new development.

Residential schools
Residential schools, as the name suggests, are establishments that provide both care services and education in the same setting. These

have traditionally served two groups of children. The first kind has a long history as former correctional facilities for wayward children. The second group – residential special schools – makes provision for children with disabilities, typically those with multiple disabilities, or with significant emotional and behavioural difficulties.

An extreme example of the first type was the *Mars* training ship, a former warship saved from the scrap yard, moored in the river Tay at Dundee between 1869 and 1929. Boys who appeared at the police court accused of petty crimes could have charges dropped in exchange for being taken to 'the *Mars*' where they had access to a curriculum that included learning trade skills such as carpentry and seamanship; music was also a big part of life (Riverside Sites, 2008). In fact, the ship provided a home for boys who were mainly destitute and abandoned, rather than offenders. It is recorded that boys from Glasgow exceeded those from Dundee, a trend for children to attend residential schools away from their home area that continues today (Watson, 2006). The late father of one of the authors used to talk of childhood memories of being threatened with being 'sent tae the *Mars*' for misbehaviour. Watson (2006) notes that the threats were still being issued by parents as recently as the 1980s, more than fifty years after the *Mars* had been towed away and scrapped! Several modern residential schools are the direct descendants of nineteenth-century reformatories, which became 'approved schools' in the early twentieth century and later 'List D' schools (referring to a now-disused government classification system).

A survey conducted for the NRCCI reported that there were thirty-one residential schools for looked after children (Hill, 2009). Additionally, there were thirteen schools providing specialist residential care facilities for children with disabilities, some of whom were also looked after. A few of these schools for children with disabilities have a national remit as they were set up to provide a specialist service for a particular group, such as Donaldson's School for the Deaf – established in 1850, originally in Edinburgh and now in Linlithgow. More recently, the National Autistic Society has established a major residential facility, Daldorch School in Catrine, Ayrshire.

There are two distinguishing features of modern, non-disability, residential schools. First, the range of specialist services offered (e.g. support for children who have experienced sexual abuse or have difficulties with substance misuse or sexually harmful behaviour, foster-care provision, short break provision) is broad and therefore each school tends to be unique. Second, the schools have adopted the standard curriculum, leading to national qualifications, though course choice may not reflect the breadth typically available in mainstream schools.

The first joint inspection of residential schools by the Care Commission and Her Majesty's Inspectorate of Education (HMIE) (the schools' inspectorate) was highly critical of care and safety in a third of schools, and found these weaknesses were paralleled by significant deficiencies in the provision of education:

> Fewer than half of schools provided a suitably broad and balanced curriculum for young people. Residential special secondary schools, where the length of the school week was less than that for mainstream schools, were unable to provide pupils with sufficient time to study or gain adequate opportunities for accreditation (Care Commission and Her Majesty's Inspectors of Schools, 2005, p. 1).

As long ago as 1976, politician and former teacher Dennis Canavan was raising concerns about residential schools being outside the local authority system. Although teachers were employed, the 'schools' tended to be run as social work establishments. The school day and week were shorter than in mainstream schools, they offered a narrow curriculum, typically with no access to formal qualifications, and teachers had no easy access to the continuing professional development provided for their mainstream peers. Although Canavan's proposal of bringing the schools into local authority control never gained much support, there have been significant improvements in respect of his criticisms in recent years. These have come about as a result of a more robust inspection regime, heightened concerns about the education and attainment of looked after children since the publication of the *Learning with Care Report* (HMI/SWSI, 2001), provision of national qualifications and the introduction of Curriculum for Excellence. The latter two developments have also enabled teachers in residential schools to participate more fully in continuing professional development.

Secure care facilities

There are two things that can be said with confidence about secure care: first, the provision has expanded considerably in recent years; second, its use is controversial (Smith and Milligan, 2005). In 2009 the seven secure care centres provided a total of 124 places. The capacity had increased by 30% in a period of six years, though this has since reduced. Some young people are placed in secure care by order of a court, following conviction for very serious offences, but most move from other placements in the care system. The requirement to lock up children implies that they are unruly and cannot be managed in open settings. There is a contrary view, which suggests that in reality it is an indictment of children's homes 'that are badly managed, poorly resourced or inadequately supported' (Smith, 2009, p. 57).

Children are placed in secure care for a range of reasons, which can include their own safety, but this is not well understood and there are widespread assumptions that all children detained in this way are offenders, typically having committed violent crimes. Aware that they sit uncomfortably within the communities where they are sited, secure care settings tend to get on with their work anonymously, a fact that adds to their isolation from mainstream society. For example, a breakout and subsequent escape of a child at one centre received widespread, critical coverage in tones that likened the facility to a prison. Yet it would be almost unknown among the wider public that secure centres are also residential 'special' schools and therefore are inspected by HMIE (see www.hmie.gov.uk to locate inspection reports).

There is an obvious tension between politicians' need to be seen to protect the public from unruly or 'difficult' children, and even to take a punitive approach to young offenders, and the welfare principles which underpin all provision for looked after children, including those who offend. In this respect, providers of secure care, and their staff, may be particularly vulnerable to political reaction about public concerns that threaten professional values and priorities (Smith and Milligan, 2005).

> Being in residential, they don't let you out, with pals, being normal and that. I think that's bad. They don't know where

you are, only down town. It's like it's better when you're locked up, they know where you are. Jails are for older people, I don't think that's right either (thirteen-year-old male) (Hill, 2009, p. 24).

A report into the use of secure care recommended a reduction in places from an average of eighteen to twelve per centre and the development of a range of community-based services with the aim of using secure provision only when absolutely necessary (SIRCC, 2009). In fact, the secure estate has mostly operated under capacity since its expansion, and in 2011 as a result of a competitive tendering process one of them was closed.

Residential care and family
The role and value of modern residential care has been repeatedly affirmed in government policy reviews, from the highly influential Skinner report (Skinner, 1992) – which described residential care as 'Another kind of home' – to the statement by the Minister for Children and Early Years in 2010 that residential care should be the 'first choice' for those children who need it (Bayes, 2009). Both these statements were intended to refute any suggestion that residential care should be viewed as a 'last resort' (Milligan and Stevens, 2006). Nevertheless the role and value of residential care have sometimes been called into question, as anything other than a last resort because of the emphasis on the *family* and *family placements* in social work policy and practice. That there is still a degree of ambivalence about the value of residential care is revealed by the fact that residential places have not been expanded during a prolonged period when the number of children becoming looked after has increased.

The emphasis on the family within social work is twofold. First, the principal aim of social work intervention (even in the context of child protection duties) is to support the birth family, so that parents can carry out their responsibilities to their children, and children are retained in their birth family. Second, since the late 1940s there has been a preference within government and the social work profession for family-type placement when children have to be taken away from the birth family. Foster placement has been preferred to small group (residential) care. While this preference has gathered widespread support, and may seem straightforward and uncontroversial, it is not without its difficulties. With respect to the first aim, there are difficulties knowing *when* to intervene in family life to protect children and especially when to take children into care – an option that also has substantial financial implications. In relation to the second aim, it should be acknowledged that not all children want to be, or can be, cared for in a family setting and so residential care remains important within the range of provision.

The priority that social workers have given to supporting birth families and returning children to the care of their parents has led to criticism of social work and other agencies in several inquiries examining cases of children killed by their parents or step-parents, after a period in care, or while under supervision by social workers (Parton, 2006). In most of these widely publicised cases it seems that social workers gave priority to the parents' wishes, or succumbed to the 'rule of optimism' concerning the progress parents were making, and were insensitive to the child or underestimated the risks the child faced being kept at home (SWIA, 2005).

In recent years increasing numbers of children are being brought into the 'looked after' system, suggesting that social work departments are more willing to remove children from their families. Local authorities face considerable cost pressures and typically employ screening measures to ensure that social workers admit a child to care only when senior managers are satisfied that all other avenues of 'home support' have been explored or are not appropriate.

Another aspect that has been reported is the tendency of social workers to be unconfident about the benefits of placing children in foster or residential care, even when the child is at serious risk in the home (Scottish Executive, 2002). This echoes an earlier finding by a parliamentary review of the out-of-home child care system in England (Great Britain, 1984), which criticised social workers for believing that admitting a child to care amounted to a failure on their part.

Social work intervention with children in Scotland is governed by the Children (Scotland) Act 1995, which prescribes 'private' family law affecting children, as well as the 'public' law context involving the intervention of social workers. In relation to children looked after away from home, the guidance accompanying the Act stresses the importance of professionals working closely with parents. Although the phrase 'partnership with parents' is not used in the guidance itself, there is considerable emphasis on professionals *communicating* with parents, *informing* them of their children's progress and *involving* them in the care process, wherever possible. This legal guidance reflected what had been widely understood as 'good practice' built up over many years. Social workers in Scotland would normally attempt to rehabilitate children with their parents when they were admitted to care. Even when it was acknowledged that children were unlikely to return home soon, there was still an expectation that residential units and foster homes would facilitate contact between parents and children.

Social work has made supporting the birth family a priority because of the idea that children need to have a long-term, permanent home in which they will grow up and which will give them a family network, vital for the development of identity, and as a practical and psychological resource throughout life. It is believed that the care system cannot ever provide that life-long commitment, even in the face of evidence from children that residential and foster placement has been a positive experience and that they have been able to keep in contact with birth parents while in care.

There has been a keen awareness of the serious deficiencies arising from a system in which children in long-term care may become completely separated from their families and leave care at around sixteen or seventeen without a sense of belonging and the support of a family network. This group are known as 'care leavers', and, while it is important not to overgeneralise and thus further stigmatise this group, many have struggled – understandably given their youth and prior history of abuse and neglect – to maintain their homes and sustain training or employment. The substantial body of research into younger care leavers has highlighted high levels of homelessness, social isolation, early pregnancy and addiction problems (Stein, 2002). On the other hand, there are research accounts that show that adult care leavers are able to develop effective relationships, sustain employment and return to education in their twenties or later, although even the most successful of them can identify continuing negative effects of their earlier experiences (Duncalf, 2010; Jahnukainen, 2007).

Social work policy has tended to promote the idea of seeking a 'permanent' alternative if a child cannot remain at home, but this is usually limited to adoption. In a policy context where only the birth family or adoption was regarded as providing the permanent family that children needed, both foster care and residential care were viewed as providing only temporary care. Even with a long-term placement where no one, including the child, contemplated a return to the birth family, the child's case continued to be reviewed as if a return home or move to permanent adoption might be possible. This left residential workers and foster carers with a dilemma: how to help children to feel settled in long-term placements when the system operated as if the placement was temporary. Carers were also discouraged from thinking of themselves as substitute parents, with all the usual parental responsibilities, including post-care involvement and commitments.

While the intention behind this approach to the use of care might seem laudable it has had negative consequences. Many children experience frequent changes of placement. There can be planned moves, from one type of placement to another, from temporary foster care back to the family home, or from temporary residential placement to foster care. There may also be unplanned moves or placement breakdowns. This pattern of movement has been characterised as 'placement instability' and reducing it has become a policy goal for governments (Bayes, 2009; DOH, 2004). It is obvious that where a child experiences several moves, sometimes in the space of a few months or disruption to an apparently settled placement, there will be negative consequences for emotional and mental well-being, schooling and the maintenance of friendships. In residential care staff will often work with children who have been repeatedly placed in unsuccessful foster placements or who have moved back and forth from home to residential or foster placement, as recurring attempts at 'rehabilitation' have failed. Poor outcomes from care are in many cases the result of system failure rather than failure of a specific placement or type of placement (Forrester, 2008).

'Homely' residential care

While the system within which residential care operates continues to be bedevilled by the problems highlighted above, the scale and characteristics of residential provision have changed markedly over the past thirty years. Until the mid-1980s the job title of residential workers was usually 'houseparent', but thereafter this term was discredited and tended to be replaced with titles such as 'residential child care officer' or more simply 'residential worker', although the term 'residential carer' is also widely used in describing work roles. The term houseparent fell out of use because greater recognition was given to the continuing role that birth parents had, both in their children's affections and also as the partners of social workers and residential carers in the care process. The term 'foster carer' was substituted for 'foster parent'. The Skinner report included 'partnership with parents' as one of its eight principles of quality residential care (Skinner, 1992).

Social work services recognised the importance of children's birth parents for a child's sense of identity, and most children in residential care, even when they remained in care on a prolonged basis, usually kept in some kind of contact with at least one parent. Importantly, local authority social work managers did not want residential workers to think of themselves as substitute parents, in the sense of directly replacing birth parents, because of a concern that if children became too attached to houseparents care would become prolonged, rather than the temporary measure they intended. Furthermore, residential workers aspired to professional status and the term 'worker' or 'officer' had higher status than the old-fashioned, more ambiguous term 'houseparent'. The change in term was thus part of the wider, modernising and professionalising agenda of the times (Edwards, 1984), and it was an attempt to be more responsive and sensitive to the parents' rights agenda, which was also being articulated.

At the same time there was a process of modernising the physical premises of residential settings; and from the late 1970s onwards there was a gradual reduction in the size of children's homes throughout the UK (Skinner, 1992; Utting, 1991). This point is explored more fully in Chapter 2. There is no doubt that these smaller homes, usually in new buildings, were a great improvement on what had gone before. Arguably the sort of care provided, what went on *in* the homes, however, was not given as much thought and attention as was put into the design of the buildings. There was some attention paid to getting homes to focus on a particular remit or purpose (Milligan, 2010), but beyond that there was little work done on models, theories or philosophies of care, even though the homes increasingly took on the most difficult or troubled adolescents. It is worth noting that at the same time as workers were advised not to think of themselves as 'parents', they were also told to make the homes more 'homely' and as much like a family environment as possible. Another change of terminology occurred when the term 'children's home' was dropped in favour of the term 'unit', signalling a change in the type of homes – from large institutions to the smaller settings – and perhaps also indicative of a place with a task, where 'work' was done, and not only somewhere for children to live.

Staff in residential care

The task of caring for children living in group settings involves addressing the normal developmental needs of children and adolescents. These include the responsibilities of parents to provide for physical and emotional needs, set boundaries, make available stimulating educational, social and cultural opportunities, and be a consistent presence in the child's life. In other respects, the work is much more complex, since most looked after children have experienced neglect and inconsistency, and some will have highly specialised needs arising from disability or past trauma and abuse.

There are at least three other ways in which the job of a residential worker is different from being a parent. First, in common with others who work with children, such as teachers, child development officers, health visitors and youth workers, the job involves developing warm but professional relationships with children. Second, the caring role is shared with other residential workers, since even in small units staff work in teams and on a rota, typically covering early, late and night shifts. The work calls for expertise in developing partnerships with a broad range of professionals providing services to children and families, often also engaging with a parent or several family members who are likely to have, or be recovering from, difficulties in their own lives.

In this respect the residential worker plays a crucial role in helping the child to manage the links between their living space, which may be temporary, and other settings, such as a parent's home, school and a therapeutic service. Third, the worker provides the link with the children's services' system, including the children's hearings administration, social work, education and health services. This aspect calls for organisational and administrative skills, particularly in managing a diary, record keeping and report writing skills. In summary, there are three aspects to the job, which might be described as direct work with children, partnership working and linking with the wider children's services system.

Despite the demanding nature of the role requirements, residential care has been typically regarded as low-status work, particularly in comparison with social work, though perceptions are changing as a result of professional registration, the introduction of specialist qualifications and the increasing adoption of theoretical frameworks to guide practice at both group and individual levels (Milligan and Furnivall, 2011).

Since 2009 it has been a statutory requirement for residential child care workers employed in Scotland to be registered with the Scottish Social Services Council (SSSC). The criteria for registration are the ability to provide evidence of 'good character' and possession of the relevant qualifications for the post. The necessary evidence of good character constitutes suitable references and the statutory requirement of background checks conducted by Disclosure Scotland under the provisions of the Protection of Vulnerable Groups (PVG) Scheme (see www.disclosurescotland.co.uk for more information). In some circumstances it is possible to be employed as a residential worker without qualifications, provided the good character aspect is satisfied and the relevant qualification is gained within a stipulated period.

A broad range of professional qualifications is recognised for work in this field, including qualified social worker, registered teacher, chartered psychologist and music therapist. There are also specialist courses in residential child care offered by further education colleges, leading to the academic qualification of Higher National Certificate (HNC) in Social Care and the Scottish Vocational Qualification (SVQ), Level 3, in Health and Social Care. Full details of the registration requirements, including additional qualifications for supervisors and managers, can be found on the SSSC website at www.sssc.uk.com. The NRCCI report recommended that from 2014 all new residential child care workers should hold a relevant child care qualification at degree or equivalent level, as well as evidence of competence in practice, though it seems unlikely that this aspiration can be achieved (Davidson *et al.*, 2009).

Residential child care draws upon knowledge and skills from other areas of practice, such as teaching, counselling and children's rights. In common with other developing professions, residential practice is also influenced by the debates and critiques emerging from a range of theoretical frameworks, including those of social work, social pedagogy, therapeutic practice, and child and youth care. These frameworks are explored in more detail within this book.

Summary

In this chapter we have introduced group or residential care within the range of settings in which children are looked after by the state in Scotland. We have considered the process whereby children come to be looked after and the types of setting in which they live. The distinctions between children's homes or units, residential schools and secure care settings were explained. We discussed the role and value of residential care and suggested that residential workers can feel frustrated because they aim to provide personalised and 'homely' care, while the system operates as if the care is provided on a temporary basis. The importance of providing nurturing experiences that respond to the developmental needs of individual children within a group setting was explored, and we discussed the implications of working simultaneously with birth parents, foster or respite carers, and other professionals. Finally, we outlined the role, training, qualifications and registration of residential workers.

Thinking outside the box

As Chapter 1 has shown, the proportion of children placed in residential care has declined at a time when there are increasing needs for 'away from home' placements. The result is that residential units tend to hold the most vulnerable, hurt or 'challenging' children who have not been able to be placed elsewhere. Such concentrations of need inevitably require high staff numbers, and thus high unit costs. Other European countries have much larger proportions of their children in residential care, while also using foster care.

Perhaps if Scottish authorities were willing to increase the numbers of residential places they would not *all* need such a high staff-to-child ratio and there would not be a proportionate increase in costs. Units with a broader range of young people and needs might well act as a more 'normalising' environment, and produce fewer placement breakdowns. The NRCCI argued tentatively that 'certain younger children [under twelve] can and do have their needs met in residential care', and 'in certain instances repeated foster care breakdowns could be avoided by earlier admission to residential care'. Perhaps – after decades of decline – all the evidence points to a need for a significant expansion of residential care places? What do you think?

What's in a name? Children in care are a group often referred to by professionals as looked after children and frequently by its abbreviation LAC. How would you like to be referred to? A plea for sensitivity in the way children are referred to is only one language issue. The changing names given to homes over the years – homes, units, houses – and the people who work in them – houseparent, residential officer, residential social worker – should also give us pause for thought. Do we uncritically accept them as 'given' and therefore legitimate? Or does language sometimes seek to cover up or hide an inconvenient truth? Does referring to a residential worker rather than a houseparent detract from their caring role? Is the term children's house less stigmatising than children's unit or children's home? What ideas lie behind the changing terminology?

Notes

1. Acts of Parliament referred to in this book can be consulted at www.legislation.gov. uk.
2. Children's statistics are published regularly by the Scottish government and can be accessed via the 'Browse statistics' area of the Scottish government website at www. scotland.gov.uk/Topics/Statistics/Browse.

CHAPTER 2

Residential Living: The Physical Environment

Introduction

In this chapter we consider the types of building and location of children's homes and residential schools, and the relationship between the nature of the living space and the care provided and experienced. We will see that some children's homes and most residential schools have long histories, while some local authority children's homes have been redeveloped or replaced over time. Residential facilities for children and young people are managed and owned by a diversity of providers: local authorities; the voluntary or charity sector, including especially the churches and religious organisations; and the private sector. We will see how ideas about what makes a place a 'home', and how reflections on how children can be offered an experience that is 'familylike', have influenced design and location.

The chapter begins with a historical perspective, examining the changing assumptions which have influenced decisions about size and location. As we shall see, these assumptions are affected by a range of influences, such as politics, economics, public opinion and theoretical perspectives. These influences are rather far removed from considerations about the purpose of group care. Furthermore, ideas emerging from the social work profession have often tended to be concerned with avoiding features of institutional care, rather than thinking positively about how to design a good small group care environment. It is appropriate, therefore, that the chapter should end with a case example that endeavours to show how clarity about the aim of care can determine the design of living space.

The influence of social work on size and location of homes

In the 1970s the tide of anti-institutionalisation coincided with the emergence of professional social workers and new social work departments, which gradually took over control of approved schools and children's homes and villages managed by the voluntary sector (Crimmens and Milligan, 2005). The over-arching policy in respect of children's services has been to seek what are called 'community-based' alternatives to residential care. It was not expected that these alternatives would completely replace residential care but that they would reduce the need for it. Meanwhile, the remaining homes became subject to debates about the type of care that should be provided – in particular, as outlined in Chapter 1, the desirability of avoiding institutionalisation and maintaining links with birth families.

Across Scotland from the late 1970s onwards, the standard local authority twenty-three-bed home was gradually phased out and replaced with eighteen-bed units; subsequently unit size was reduced to ten beds or fewer. One of the authors was the 'officer-in-charge' of a twenty-three-bed unit in Glasgow which was closed at the end of the 1980s and replaced with a ten-bed unit and another five-bed unit. The aim was to make the homes more 'normal' and less 'institutional', and this was understood to relate mainly to the *location* – placed in residential areas alongside other domestic homes – and the *size* of the homes, making them smaller and more familial and replacing shared bedrooms with single-occupancy ones. Residential workers, while unhappy about the sharp reduction in the overall size of the residential sector, mainly agreed about the desirability of reducing the size of individual units, and moving away from dormitories in schools and large, shared bedrooms in children's homes.

There have however been negative consequences of the shift to smaller homes. Small units tend to be less flexible in making accommodation available, and this can make it more difficult to match children to the most suitable placement and can prevent siblings from being accommodated together. The existence of small units has also in some instances blurred the distinction between foster care and residential care, as some foster carers take three or more children into their own home.

The promotion of family life, and the desire to see residential placement as temporary, and not replacing the child's birth family, has also influenced considerations of location. Social work managers usually wanted to avoid placing children far away from their home areas, which would make maintaining contact with their birth family difficult and expensive. They preferred to place children in typical residential neighbourhoods where they could mix with other children. Because of the urban–rural spread of Scotland's population, and the diverse size of local authorities, the notion of closeness to a local community is variable, especially for children who may need intensive therapy or other specialist care. Location may also depend on the willingness of communities and elected members to accept a children's home.

Market forces have also played a part in the geography of provision as private sector providers have responded to government policy promoting the development of a 'mixed economy of care', encouraging local authorities to enter into contracts with private and not-for-profit providers. Some private providers have specialised in placements for (older) children with significant difficulties or in crisis and for whom local authorities cannot make suitable support arrangements either in their own services or in a voluntary-sector residential school. These are usually small homes with provision for one to three children. Most are situated in rural areas, the locations probably reflecting lower property prices and the prior existence of a provider in the area. They have the advantage of being places where children can be supervised more easily and generally without conflict with neighbours.

These rural locations also help to isolate children from harmful associations or anti-social peer groups, with freedom in which to develop their identity and make new friendships. But there are problems associated with children being geographically separated from their birth families and familiar social networks, ones to which they will ultimately return. Moreover the placement of children away from their home local authority can cause problems in accessing suitable education, particularly if a child has significant additional support needs. Nevertheless, social workers may consider the respite offered by a more rural location provides a therapeutic setting in which advantages outweigh the disadvantages. This may be especially true for children and young people with the most severe difficulties, for whom it can be difficult to find a stable and containing placement. The changes in size and location of homes suggest a lack of consensus about what constitutes the ideal or most suitable placement for different needs in residential care. The existence of thirty-two local authorities responsible for services also means that there has been no central or regional co-ordination of the development of the sector since local government reorganisation in 1996.

In the section that follows we provide a brief overview of the changes in residential care provision – homes, schools, disability services – over time to help the reader understand how the sector has developed.

Historical overview
1970s to 1990s – Children's homes
The Social Work (Scotland) Act 1968 led to the development of generic social work departments in 1969 and the setting up of the children's hearing system in 1971. The social work service was set up as a family service, a 'one-stop shop' open to all. This new service incorporated the previously separate departments for children, welfare, probation and court, and hospital social work. In respect of children in trouble or in need, social workers were expected to work to keep children in their families wherever possible. Admission to care would be contemplated in cases that were more exceptional or urgent. Social workers were to undertake investigation and assessments of the referrals to a children's hearing and provide the supervision and arrange placements following a hearing. Social workers were also to prepare the review reports on the basis of which the hearings would subsequently decide whether children remained in care or went home.

When first established, these social work departments were the responsibility of fifty-two local authorities of different kinds, including cities, large burghs and counties. The first years were concerned with developing new systems, and the residential sector did not immediately undergo major change (Murphy, 1992).

After local government reorganisation in 1975, the new regional councils with their large social work departments created a new context for children in care. In tandem with the plans to increase the number of children in foster care, the existing stock of children's homes and residential schools was viewed critically. With a newly professionalised workforce and the growing size of social work departments, social work managers wanted to create alternatives to residential care. To be able to direct children to these alternatives they also needed control over admission to and discharge from residential facilities so that children could be rehabilitated more quickly. This contrasted with the previous situation in which the heads of homes or schools had considerable influence over admission and discharge. Local authority social workers were now expected to provide increased support to vulnerable families and to engage with children in trouble with the law, in order to prevent admission to out-of-home care whenever possible. They were also expected to work to reintegrate children with their families when the children had spent time in care.

Local authorities developed or refurbished their own children's homes, and this reduced their reliance on voluntary-sector homes, such as Quarrier's, Barnardo's and Aberlour. Some old villas were modernised, but from the late 1980s there was a policy in some local authorities to provide homes in the areas from which many of the children came. Some children's homes were built in areas of multiple-deprivation, particularly in the west of Scotland within the former Strathclyde Regional Council area between 1975 and 1996. These locations met the aim of providing children's homes near to children's family homes, but the idealism did not match the realities of the effects of poverty. Most of these homes were subsequently closed, as the social difficulties of the neighbourhoods led to the buildings, and the children within them, becoming the target of hostility. Since then local authorities have experimented with locations for new homes, generally trying to keep them close to areas where many of the children come from, but carefully choosing areas on the edges of well-established housing developments, and in more mixed or relatively prosperous places.

1970s to 1990s – Homes for children with disabilities
At the start of this period, children with disabilities who were taken into hospital or care typically remained there for long periods, often

for their whole childhood. By the end of the 1980s the situation had changed considerably. Pressure for better support for children within families and for improved education for children with disabilities meant it was no longer considered acceptable for children to live in large institutional-type care or long-stay hospitals. For those few children who could not be looked after at home, various forms of special fostering, including 'shared care', were developed. At the start of the period there were homes for children with disabilities within the large village communities such as Quarrier's, Aberlour and Smyllum. Some large homes catered solely for children with disabilities, such as East Park Home in Glasgow. The village homes closed, while the larger homes reduced the size of their residential units and gradually also developed 'respite homes' in the community. The main campus of these homes typically remained in use, though mainly for education and recreation rather than living space. Some children with less severe or complex disabilities were also placed in 'mainstream' residential homes. There were also the national schools for children with specific conditions, notably the Royal School for the Blind and Donaldson's School for the Deaf, both in Edinburgh but accommodating children from the whole of Scotland. Many of the children in these schools were not legally 'looked after', and most would return home at weekends.

1970s to 1990s – The residential schools
The residential school sector was influenced by the same general trends of reduction and redevelopment as were affecting the rest of the residential sector in this period. The largest group of schools was known as 'approved' schools until the reforms brought in by the Social Work (Scotland) Act 1968 and the setting up of the children's hearing system. The schools had been used mainly for offenders, though children could also be placed on 'care or protection' grounds: for example, if they had been the victims of offences of child abuse or neglect.

With the advent of the children's hearing system in 1971 the schools, which were mostly owned and managed by the voluntary sector, were integrated into the child care system and renamed 'List D' schools (referring to a now-redundant government category system).

The schools continued to be funded by central government but had their own boards of management. Responsibility for placing children passed to the children's hearing system, and the children brought into the care system were now supervised by social workers. There was a prolonged period of tension between the schools' boards and the local authorities over the role of the schools in a new system which was moving away from using residential care. In 1986 funding from central government finally stopped and was transferred to the local authorities. At this point they became known, along with the remaining 'special needs' schools, simply as 'residential schools'. The number of List D schools had reduced from twenty-six to fourteen between 1979 and 1986 as a result of:

> a decrease in demand for residential school places caused in part by demographic factors and in part by an increasing willingness on the part of placing authorities to develop and use alternative community resources such as intermediate treatment or community carers, as well as increasing use of children's homes for children subject to compulsory supervision (McCracken, 1992, p. 111).

Some schools entered into 'user agreements' with local authorities, which assumed funding. Some were fully taken over by one local authority, while the remainder continued either as voluntary-sector institutions or in private ownership. Some focused entirely on children with 'special needs'. While the residential school sector as a whole was contracting, paradoxically the number of secure units increased, albeit from a very small base (Smith and Milligan, 2005).

The current picture

Since the mid-1990s the average size of children's homes has continued to reduce as providers have attempted to create care environments that are domestic rather than institutional in character, and to maximise the child's privacy. This aim has led to the provision of single rooms as standard and increasingly also to the inclusion of en-suite bathrooms. The result of such improvement in facilities, nevertheless, has been to produce a perverse kind of institutionalisation, in the sense that few ordinary family homes have an en-suite bedroom for each child.

Other aspects of home design have been influenced by ideas about how much space should be given over to the staff. Typically, there is an office for the manager, which is sometimes shared with other workers, or there may be a second office for the staff to work in when they are undertaking tasks such as record keeping, writing reports and phoning social workers and family members. The matter of whether a separate room should be provided for meetings and visits, or whether that is too 'institutional', has led to different solutions in different homes. There is no consensus about what is the best design for a small children's home, and in fact the design, the amount of money spent on building and fitting-out, and the physical size and layout of new homes vary considerably across Scotland.

Similar trends can be seen in the residential school sector. More schools have closed, and those remaining have reduced in capacity and accommodated the children in small units on the campus in place of previously large buildings. The residential accommodation in the schools is now very much like those of small children's homes.

Design considerations
There has been little research about the application of good design principles in creating homes for children. There is at least agreement among professionals about the importance of the living environment in showing respect for children and giving them the message that they are valued. Standard five of the *National Care Standards, Care Homes for Children and Young People* states: 'you should stay in a warm, welcoming and comfortable environment' (Scottish Executive, 2005).

It is widely understood that children should be able to personalise their living space through choice of decor, posters, duvet covers and family photographs. Little attention has traditionally been given to a more holistic approach to the application of interior design in creating a therapeutic environment. One exception is a study of the refurbishment of children's homes conducted by South Lanarkshire Council, which made use of the expertise of interior design consultants (Docherty *et al.*, 2006). The design of homes has usually been driven by statutory requirements and health and safety considerations, rather than the purpose of child care. The importance of the physical milieu has begun to receive attention in the literature in relation to educational and medical settings (e.g. Maggie's Cancer Caring Centres), but so far there has been little impact in relation to residential child care. Thinking about design options also creates invaluable opportunities for consulting with children and involving them in influencing the final plans. We return to the matter of design later in this chapter, when we introduce a case study example where the purpose of residential care influenced the design of new children's houses.

National standards and independent inspection

A national system of independent inspection of all care services was introduced in 2002, replacing a system in which local authority inspection staff had inspected residential homes in their area. The new system was based on *National Care Standards*, which applied throughout Scotland. The standards are written in the language of service users and from their perspective: for example: 'you should stay in a friendly and welcoming environment that is warm and comfortable' (Scottish Executive, 2005, p. 14).

Some evidence about improving physical environment standards can be found by comparing two summary reports from the Care Commission on various aspects of care in relation to the *National Care Standards* (Care Commission, 2004; 2010). A direct comparison between the two reports is not possible because of changes in the inspection methodology, including a system of grading that was introduced in 2008. The 2004 summary report quantifies the number of 'requirements' (mandatory notices) and 'recommendations' (advisory notices) imposed on children's homes. Inspectors' concerns raised about buildings are frequently stipulated as requirements; in 14% of cases (the second highest proportion) the report recorded failings in the 'fitness of premises, such as poor internal and external lighting' (Care Commission, 2004, p. 26) or included recommendations about the need to 'refurbish and upgrade buildings' (ibid., p. 27) . By 2010 the summary report indicated that 88% of all homes were achieving grades 4–6 on a six-point scale (where four is 'good', five is 'very good' and six is 'excellent'). Other reviews in recent years have been more concerned with matters such as emergency admissions, hasty care-leaving, lack of education support, neglect of mental health, and training of care staff (Bayes, 2009; SIRCC, 2006).

To summarise, local authorities now tend to have small units located within or adjacent to stable and relatively prosperous residential communities. Voluntary and private sector schools and the newer specialist services are often located in rural or edge-of-town areas. 'User agreements', developed to a limited extent from the mid-1980s, did not survive the reorganisation of local government in 1996. Since then the absence of 'commissioning' or co-ordinated planning, at either national or regional level, means that services have developed in an *ad hoc* way. It is obviously not possible to have highly specialist services for the most challenging children located in or near to all of Scotland's thirty-two local authorities. Further aspects of the interaction between local authorities are explored in the following section.

Placement policies and practice

Broad policy aspirations, such as placing children near their home areas, can mask significant differences in the needs of individual children and the requirement to match them with the placements that are available. Children are sometimes placed at a distance from home when social workers have to find a 'bed' for a child at short notice and accept a place where one can be found (Milligan *et al.*, 2006). This situation has developed partly as a result of an increase in the number of children becoming looked after, and partly because local authorities have reduced their stock of children's homes and now rarely have spare capacity to allow any kind of matching in practice.

There are occasions – exceptions perhaps – where a local authority will prefer to place a child some distance from the family home: for example, where an adolescent is experiencing turmoil, characterised by offending behaviour or association with other young people involved in anti-social behaviour. In such circumstances, placement in a residential school with experience of dealing with challenging young offenders is often a preferred choice, even if the plan indicates the need for only a brief period of care. Similarly, if a child has been disruptive and cannot be supported within a children's home a move to another home in the same authority may be contemplated. In small local authorities this option may not be possible, and an independent-sector placement, perhaps at a distance, may seem the best, or only, option. A similar tension between placement ideals and practice exists in relation to foster care. A local authority will try to recruit local carers but will usually accept carers who live some distance away, and retain those who move in order to maintain their pool of carers and to provide stability for children already in placement.

Thus the ideal of placing children close to their birth family and community cannot always be realised in practice. There are also questions about how reasonable this aspiration is. If highly specialist services are needed for a relatively small number of children, and at times on a short-term basis, these cannot be available in every part of Scotland. To move towards a more rational distribution of services would require a high degree of co-operation between local authorities as well as long-term financial partnership with voluntary-sector or private providers. It is not clear if the 'levers' exist that will require councils to operate in this way. Despite concerns about the current location of units, local authorities have not taken the initiative to enter into such long-term arrangements. The regulatory body has, however, now demanded action on planning and provided guidance on the commissioning of services (SWIA, 2009).

The matter of costs is complex, and many local authorities do not know accurately the full costs of their services (Audit Scotland, 2010). There is no evidence that independent sector costs are actually higher than those of local authorities. While local authorities may want to retain expenditure in-house, this aspiration is constrained by the fact that the independent sector continues to provide placements for many children with the most significant needs.

The independent sector is often seen as a last resort and expensive, and therefore the primary driver for managers of local authority children's services is to reduce use of residential placement. Planning to use such placements – even though they have always been part of the child care sector – has been resisted. In a climate of reductions in social service spending, the first aim for many local authorities is to reduce reliance on non-council-run services.

To summarise, while there is considerable agreement about the preferred size of homes, there continues to be a wide diversity of locations and a lack of co-ordinated planning of services by groups of local authorities. The process of commissioning of services based on joint planning between purchasers and providers is progressing slowly.

Creating a children's house

The case study in this section is based on the experience of one local authority, North Lanarkshire Council, which worked with GCA Architecture+Design consultancy on the designs for five new children's 'houses' in a process involving consultations with children, residential care workers, managers, elected members and the community. We have reproduced (Figure 2.1) an architect's plan drawing of one of the houses. Each of the five designs is unique, responding to features in the locality (for example, one was located in a conservation village), with later designs incorporating details as a result of learning from the experience of living in the earlier-built homes.

The local authority had inherited from its predecessor, Strathclyde Regional Council, homes built to a design of the 1960s, influenced by a modular approach to architecture which dominated public housing, hospitals and institutions of the time. Their design featured rectangular rooms and corridors that could be scaled up or down as required. The considerations were, variously, numbers of children to be accommodated (typically twenty-three at this time), cost and building efficiency. The design was influenced by space and cost considerations rather than an understanding of the relationship between building and purpose. The result in the eyes of children and staff was a brutal industrial appearance, and fabric that was not respected and easily damaged. Sadly, the atmosphere of depression unwittingly created matched the mood of children who had been removed to a place of safety from unhappy home circumstances.

The North Lanarkshire children's house of 2009 incorporated characteristics into the design that were the product of a clearer view of its purpose. The creative process involved three interconnected elements: a brief, based on the collective experience of senior staff; translation of the concept of 'safe care' and the service to be provided into a building design; and consultations with young people, local politicians and residents. One of the senior managers described the process to the authors in 2011:

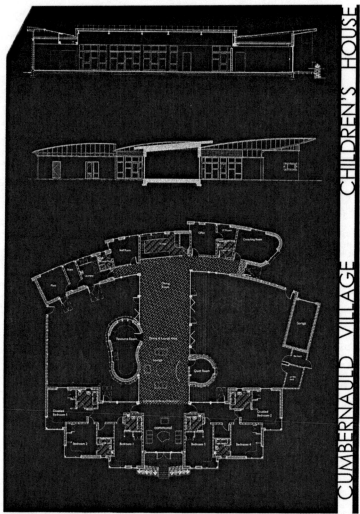

CUMBERNAULD VILLAGE   CHILDREN'S HOUSE

Figure 2.1 Plan of a children's house. (Reproduced by permission of GCA Architecture + Design and North Lanarkshire Council.)

We used all of our knowledge to develop two to three pages of script to offer to GCA [the architects] that would enable them to get an idea of what we, as residential care managers, meant when were talking about a therapeutic environment … A therapeutic environment is a building that actually helps the staff to deliver the outcomes that they are trying to achieve and so every element of the building in terms of

> living, playing, activity, eating, feeding, sleeping, going to
> the bathroom, managing the home, all had to be thought in
> terms of how does their role relate to what is going on in the
> building and how are staff able to guarantee that six young
> people … could live in safe care in a building that does not
> look institutional.

Three aspects of the creative process serve to give a fascinating insight into the interface between the design of the house and its function as a residential home for looked after children. One was an exhibition of the proposed design, using architectural models and plans, which ran for a month. A range of stakeholders, including young people, residential workers, managers, elected members and police officers, was actively encouraged to visit the exhibition and to engage with the proposal by completing a questionnaire and writing on 'post-it' slips. The design was modified as a result of the feedback.

Another aspect was a workshop for residential managers at which two criticisms were made of the plan: the managers thought the office was too small; and they felt the proposal to have a kitchen designed as the centre of the house with free access to all should be revised in favour of a functional kitchen, which could be locked. These concerns get to the heart of understanding the function of a children's house: it is essentially a community where the opportunities for adults and young people to develop supportive, nurturing relationships are maximised. The planning group involved in the design of the new house believed firmly that the therapeutic model they envisaged, dependent on residential workers spending the maximum time possible engaging directly with children, would have been compromised by having an office large enough for staff to congregate in and a kitchen shut off to children. The group's vision was ultimately supported.

A third aspect was the fire and rescue department's view that the lack of a corridor into which bedrooms opened with a route to a fire exit presented a sufficient concern to prevent the building gaining a fire safety certificate. As the plan shows, the design concept featured a central living space, flowing into private courtyards and bedrooms placed at the opposite end from office and kitchen to create privacy. The architects were able to overcome the fire department's concerns with modifications to the design in a way that did not compromise the care-led principles. The local authority also played its part in backing the principles, since the modifications increased the final cost of the £2.5 million building.

The architects responded to their brief by creating an open-plan, multi-purpose space with bedrooms accessed directly off this space. The design considerations allowed for space to provide for facilities such as computers and to encourage participation in activities such as art, music and games. The aim was to create comfortable areas where young people could relax without feeling they were being supervised at all times. This clever combination of privacy within an open-plan area is illustrated in Figure 2.2. It also shows the use of light combined with high-quality furnishings, which produce an environment that

Figure 2.2 Images of activity space in a children's house. (Photographs: Graham Connelly with kind permission of North Lanarkshire Council.)

aims to express how children are valued. The importance of being engaged in activity is also reflected in an outdoor courtyard-style garden, where a small, kick-about pitch, basketball area and decked area provide for a range of outdoor activities.

Summary

This chapter has highlighted the importance of understanding the relationship between the aims of residential care and the living space in which this is provided. The historical perspective showed the trend towards smaller houses for about six children, with en-suite study-bedrooms, from the large mansions requisitioned as orphanages for up to a hundred or more children of the nineteenth and early twentieth centuries, through the modular buildings of the 1960s, accommodating around twenty children, to the present-day concern to ensure that function influences design.

Thinking outside the Box

Using the plan of the North Lanarkshire children's house (Figure 2.1) as the starting point for your ideas, imagine you are a participant in the consultation about the design proposal.

How might building design help with such considerations as children's education, health and emotional well-being? What other considerations, beyond building design, would contribute to looked after young people's development as safe, healthy, achieving, nurtured, active, respected, responsible and included individuals?

What are the considerations in relation to the location of a children's house and how might these impact on safe care? (Hint: you might consider family contact, school attendance and many other factors.)

CHAPTER 3

Children's Stories and Children's Views

Introduction

In this chapter we have set ourselves three aims. First, we want to help the reader understand the role of residential care in providing a home for children and young people. Second, we outline different ways in which children's views about their experiences of living in residential care are gathered and articulated, principally on their behalf by advocacy and campaigning organisations, but also by service users themselves. Finally, we consider the extent to which these views are represented in research and policy development.

Children's stories

We begin this section with two case examples. These accounts are based on real cases, but some details, including names, have been changed to protect the identities of the individuals portrayed. In the first example – that of David – the placement lasted for three months before the young person was able to return home to his family. This relatively short episode of being looked after is not typical. In 2011 8% of all looked after children in Scotland were looked after for between six weeks and six months, while the modal period for a continuous episode of care (for 40%) was between one and three years (Scottish Government, 2012a).

David

David was thirteen when he was placed in a local authority children's unit. He was living with his mother, Alice, and three younger siblings: Holly (six), Amanda (eight) and Kelly (eleven). The family had been known to social workers for some time, but growing concerns about Alice's deteriorating mental health and use of alcohol led to a child protection conference being called and the decision that the children needed to be removed from a situation where they were felt to be at risk of neglect. Unfortunately, no placement could be found that would accommodate all four children, and this led to the family being split up, with David going to live in a residential setting and the girls being placed with a foster carer.

David enjoyed school and had near-perfect attendance. While he found the circumstances leading to the family break-up very difficult to accept, he was pleased that the care arrangements meant his family were at least living close by and that he could stay at the high school where he had friends and where, by his own account, he was 'doing really well'. But David did not settle easily in the children's unit and was very obviously unhappy and angry. He felt he had little in common with the other young people, some of whom had made unfriendly comments about his diligence in doing homework. As a result, David preferred to spend long periods in his room, and staff became concerned about his moodiness and unwillingness to engage with them. The local authority had facilities for children looked after away from home to access an independent advocacy service, so they could talk through feelings about their care with a trained worker not employed by the council. Staff arranged for advocacy worker, Mandy, to visit David at the unit.

As they chatted together, getting to know each other, Mandy quickly realised that David was highly articulate and had reflected intelligently on the family's circumstances. He had no difficulty putting into words his feelings about the break-up of his family, but he had a high level of maturity, which meant he was able both to understand the concerns of professionals about his mother's capacity to care for her children and also to question the practical arrangements made by social workers. Mandy learned that David had been used to caring for his mother and younger sisters: for example, going shopping, making meals and helping to get the younger girls out to school. While David understood the concerns social workers had about the family's welfare, and he was relieved that his mother was now getting treatment for her depression and addiction problems, he also felt strongly that the importance of the role he had played in keeping the family together had not been properly recognised by the professionals – it was as if this role had been abruptly taken away from him. He felt he was the expert on his family's situation, but that no one had asked his opinion on what kind of support they needed. David believed he was not being given credit for his awareness of his mother's caring qualities, as well as her obvious difficulties in looking after herself and her children.

Another major concern David expressed related to the limited contact he had with his sisters and the fact that his contact visits with his mother were supervised, something he felt did not take account of his maturity and also made him feel as if he was not being trusted. Mandy explained to David that he could request a children's hearing to review the care arrangements, and together they worked on making the application and also rehearsing what David planned to say to the panel members. Meanwhile Mandy discovered that workers were concerned that David's monthly visits to see his sisters were unsettling the girls who became distressed when they saw their brother. She was able to persuade staff that the distress would dissipate if contact was more regular and more natural.

Mandy accompanied David to his review to give him moral support, but she did not need to speak to the panel because David articulated his concerns confidently and explained clearly what he hoped to get from the meeting. As a result, contact with his siblings was increased to fortnightly (with the provision of increasing this to weekly visits). The panel also agreed with David's argument that there was no risk in having unsupervised visits to see Alice, and that being able to see her regularly would put his mind at rest and help him to settle better in the children's unit. The unit was within walking distance of the family home and David soon got into a pattern of visiting his mum on most days, usually on his way home from school.

Alice's treatment programme progressed well and her health improved. The social work department made arrangements for support to be provided in the house. At a children's hearing it was decided that it was safe for the family to be reunited – first David returned home and then, after a few weeks, the girls were brought back.

Just over one year later, Alice became very drunk one night and David phoned the social work out-of-hours' service requesting help. As a result of this incident, a child protection referral was made and a case conference arranged. David asked Mandy if she would again help him to prepare for the meeting. Once again, David made an articulate presentation. He pointed out that he was attending school and continuing to do well, and had ambitions for his future. 'This is my family', he said, 'and we've been coping. I feel I've been punished because I phoned social work.' The outcome of the case conference was that the children were not placed on the child protection register, though home support was continued.

In contrast to David's short-term episode of care, the second case example – that of Kirsty – illustrates the all-too-common experience of a young person looked after over a period of many years with a great number of placement moves.

Kirsty

Kirsty had been well known to the social work department of her local authority for a long time. She presented to workers as a very angry girl, openly hostile to most people who came into contact with her. Kirsty was first placed in foster care at age ten after her father left home and her mother's health deteriorated. There then followed a series of foster placements, all of which broke down, apparently because of challenging behaviour which carers found impossible to manage. Kirsty next had a period of her life in which she moved frequently between placements: going from a children's unit to a residential school, then on to another children's unit, followed by a spell of shuttling between various residential units.

Then, aged fifteen, Kirsty arrived at a children's home after a spell in secure care and met staff who were determined they would end the pattern of discontinuity. The workers saw a physically mature teenager, angry at the world, but nevertheless anxious to be loved. Kirsty's need for intimacy had led her to make inappropriate relationships; she was promiscuous and was known to have been involved on the fringes of prostitution. The residential workers began to learn more about Kirsty's family world, one in which the care system featured significantly. Kirsty's father had been in care, and his children with another partner were also being looked after by the local authority. Kirsty was angry with her parents, particularly with her mum, Liz, who she saw as putting herself first and 'not going out on a limb' for her daughter. There was no obvious intimacy between mother and daughter, and their relationship was characterised by an atmosphere of aggression and recrimination. Liz was constantly critical of Kirsty's appearance, saying she looked like a prostitute, though the actual language she used was more graphic. As if to fulfil her mother's negative image of her, Kirsty's behaviour was putting her at risk, and her anger caused problems at school, at home and in the community.

Of the first fifteen days Kirsty was living in the residential unit, staff had no knowledge of her whereabouts for about half this time. Inevitably she was detained on a secure warrant, but this time a worker from the home accompanied Kirsty to the secure unit and then visited her regularly during her time there – an experience she had not come across before. This time she knew that she would be going back to the children's home to stay with workers who were not going to give up on her.

The worker, Andy, made weekly visits, which were a mixture of social contact and opportunities for more therapeutic work. This involved talking about what had led up to the present, acknowledging the difficulties and considering what, working together, they could do about these. The discussions included talking through Kirsty's feelings about her mum and also about her self-image. During one of these discussions Kirsty announced, 'You know I'm good with kids. I looked after my dad's kids when they were babies.' Andy said they hadn't known this, but the insight provided by Kirsty herself was the breakthrough needed to begin acknowledging other things she was good at. The explanation Kirsty had been given for being placed in secure care was that she would not be 'safe' otherwise. Andy now presented her with a challenge: 'We are not going to *make* you safe, but we do want you to be safe enough so you don't have to be in secure care, and can come and stay with us.' Kirsty was being given the chance to show she could be trusted to create her own boundaries.

The transition from secure care to the open setting of the residential unit was gradual, beginning with weekend visits. On the first of these, Kirsty went missing for four hours but returned herself. Workers were careful to reinforce the 'returning' behaviour rather than the absconding. Kirsty's progress was endorsed by children's panel members when a review hearing decided to make the return to the unit permanent. Andy said: 'We told the panel we wanted her, and she wants to be with us.'

Kirsty stayed at the residential unit for a further year before she left care as she approached her seventeenth birthday. She had met Don and they began a relationship. It was obvious to staff that Kirsty was happy and they could see that the relationship was not exploitative. Andy visited Don at home and they had an open discussion about the implications of Kirsty's looked after status for their relationship. Some years later the couple have children together, and they keep in touch with Andy and his colleagues.

Commentary

Both of these accounts are based on interviews the authors conducted with workers who knew the young people well. They are intended to help the reader to understand the circumstances that lead young people to residential care and to give a true sense of the care experience. Both cases had positive outcomes and therefore challenge the general picture of the predictability of poor outcomes for children in residential care.

The stereotype of public care as inevitably bad for children has been challenged by, among others, Donald Forrester, who with colleagues conducted a review of the research on the impact of care for children in England and Wales (Forrester *et al.*, 2009). While the researchers could identify only twelve studies of this type, and that poverty of inquiry itself tells a story, the research reviewed 'consistently found that children entering care tended to have serious problems but that in general their welfare improved over time' (ibid., p. 439). The authors point out that their finding is consistent with those in other countries and argue that it has important policy implications, in particular: 'it suggests that attempts to reduce the use of public care are misguided, and may place more children at risk of serious harm' (ibid., p. 439).

The value of case studies is that they are meant to typify the group being studied, and they can highlight common features of experience. However, since they represent real lives and illustrate different personal circumstances, they are also a reminder of the importance of understanding individual differences and translating empathy for young people's unique experience into care practice. Such understanding is the basis of developing positive relationships between residential staff and young people – what the Skinner report describes as 'fundamental to all aspects of residential care, including setting limits to behaviour' (Skinner, 1992). Mark Smith makes the point that the close and caring relationships that workers develop with children in residential settings have to be negotiated with a sensitivity that is supportive but, for example, 'does not eclipse the potential for a child to rebuild and/or maintain loving attachments with parents' (Smith, 2009, p. 122).

The case studies, though real, are effectively second-hand accounts, mediated through the reflections of the workers who recounted them. There is no reason to believe the accounts are inaccurate, but they are inevitably nuanced by workers' adult-oriented observations. For that reason, it is vital to have access to the perspectives of children and young people about residential care. The importance of providing opportunities for children to have their say about their care experiences is recognised formally in care standards that are now commonly used by inspection agencies and audit services in many countries to assess the quality of care provided. They are also intended to help individual service users determine their rights and, if necessary, to make complaints about their care experience. For example, Standard eighteen of the *National Care Standards* states: 'The care home welcomes your views so they can continuously improve the quality of services. Staff encourage you to give your views and suggestions, whether positive or negative' (Scottish Government, 2005, p. 43).

Most agencies will have formal arrangements for children and young people to express their opinions, using a range of methods, including local inspection, independent advocacy and speak-out conventions as well as by creative means, such as drama and artwork. An example of the latter is *Reflections + Visions: The World Through Different Eyes*, a youth participation project organised by the Voice of Reason group in Aberdeen and Who Cares? Scotland, in which nine young people worked with a professional photographer to create images that encapsulated their 'journey through care' experiences

(SIRCC, 2010b). The report containing the images is available online at www.celcis.org. In one dramatic image Jordan is shown looking pensively through a smashed pane of glass, a tear flowing down his cheek:

> This picture was to show that young people's life in care can often be not great and sometimes shatters young people's lives. I want you to look at my eyes in the picture and for you to ask yourself: What is life really like for a young person in care? How would you feel? What can you do to stop shattering young people's hopes and dreams (SIRCC, pp. 10–11)?

Adrian Ward points out that: 'No specific method or combination of methods will in itself create a system of open communication and power-sharing: what is needed is the creation of ... the right culture or "atmosphere" in which people will be listened to' (Ward, 2007, p. 48). Ward observes that, while the responsibility for creating the atmosphere in which open communication can take place lies principally with managers and the staff team, it is more likely to occur where individual workers pay 'meticulous attention to clients' views and needs during everyday interactions' and demonstrate 'a concern to respond constructively to requests and complaints' (ibid., p. 49).

Advocacy organisations
In the first case example presented earlier in this chapter, David was supported by an independent advocate to make his feelings about his loss of role as a carer for his family known to children's panel members and to have his insight into his mother's strengths and needs taken seriously. Independent advocacy is usually provided by third-sector organisations, i.e. the charity sector. One such charity is Who Cares? Scotland, which has its origin in responses to an influential report published by the National Children's Bureau, *Who Cares? Young People in Care Speak Out* (Paige and Clark, 1977). Formed in 1978, Who Cares? Scotland began when young people in care got together to share their experiences in meetings facilitated by supportive adults. Events held in different parts of Scotland followed from the success of local activity and through these events young people in care found a voice that was influential in, for example,

developing a charter of rights for young people in care, and contributing significantly to *Another Kind of Home* (Skinner, 1992), the Children (Scotland) Act 1995, and publishing consultation reports on matters raised by young people. For example, the *Let's Face It!* report identified concerns of young people in residential care, of which feeling safe and protected were found to be the most important (Paterson *et al.*, 2003; Watson, 2004). Who Cares? Scotland has been a partner in SIRCC and more recently the Centre for Excellence for Looked After Children in Scotland (CELCIS).

In 1988 Who Cares? Scotland secured funding to employ two development officers to work across Scotland. By 2012 it had more than forty staff members, of whom most were engaged in providing advocacy services directly to children looked after in most of Scotland's thirty-two local authorities. Although the organisation has grown in scale and its approaches have changed over the years, the values and aims have remained virtually the same. For example, the charity's board and committees include looked after young people or care leavers, as well volunteers co-opted for their specialist expertise in charity governance matters, maintaining the important principle of young people and adults working together:

> Who Cares? Scotland's mission is to provide an active voice for all of Scotland's children and young people in care. Every day we work hard to deliver the best quality independent advocacy service to our young people so that they can achieve their full potential. We ensure their rights are realised, their needs satisfied and their achievements recognised. We do this by working with young people themselves, by campaigning for change and by offering advice to national and local government.
>
> Our organisation's values reflect our mission and aims. We listen to and respect children and young people's views and are confident in their abilities. We take a caring, supportive approach to helping our children and young people. We are trustworthy, honest and reliable in all that we do. We respect human rights and promote positive attitudes, views and behaviours towards children and young people in care.

>   We're an ambitious organisation, and we're building
>   on our successes. We are continually modernising, and we
>   actively look for opportunities to develop and extend our
>   services. By always aiming higher we can campaign for even
>   more positive changes and speak out ever more clearly for
>   our looked after children (see www.whocaresscotland.org).

An example of the charity's campaigning work can be found in
the report prepared for its thirtieth anniversary, *Caring About Success*
(Siebelt *et al.*, 2008), which presented the findings of a consultation
with young people about how they defined success and how their
achievements were recognised and ambitions encouraged. One of the
recommendations of the report called on the Scottish government
and its partners to:

>   launch a national campaign aimed at dispelling the myths
>   associated with being in care and to promote positive
>   images of children and young people looked after away
>   from home, including the message that they are children
>   and young people first and foremost (Siebelt *et al.*, p. 45).

The recommendation was accepted, and a media and advertising
campaign, using the slogan *Give Me a Chance: Be Fair to a Child in
Care* was carried out during 2010 and 2011. The images used in the
campaign and further information can be viewed on the campaign
website at www.givemeachancescotland.org.

After many years of the rights of children in care settings being
formalised in care standards, which are largely based on the United
Nations Convention on the Rights of the Child (United Nations,
1989), it is useful to reflect on the atmosphere of the late 1970s that
helped to establish Who Cares? Scotland as well as its sister organisations in the other nations of the UK. Mike Stein identifies a range
of influences, including the growth from the late 1960s of pressure
groups such as Shelter and the Child Poverty Action Group, and a
reaction against the casework approach of child care officers:

>   ... and their preoccupation with individual problems and
>   solutions. Advocacy, welfare rights, group and community
>   work were increasingly seen as relevant to the plight of 'clients'

confronted with a range of social problems, including poverty,
homelessness and inner-city deprivation (Stein, 2012, p. 5).

Despite this long and impressive history of campaigning, the need
to speak out for children and young people in care has not dimin-
ished. Some more recent examples of concerns raised about the
rights of children in care to experience a normal childhood include
the reports *Sweet 16?* highlighting the high proportion of children
who leave care at age sixteen (Scotland's Commissioner for Children
and Young People, 2008) and *Go Outdoors!*, which shows how mis-
understandings about risk assessment can make residential workers
overly cautious about allowing children to take part in routine outdoor activities (SIRCC, 2010a).

Children's views in research and policy development

One way in which the children's rights movement has ensured that
looked after children and young people can air their views about
their care is through research and its subsequent dissemination in
reports, journal articles and conference presentations. Research is
typically conducted by professionals, generally employed by universities and research institutes. A less common form of research is that
conducted by service users themselves, usually with the support of
experienced researchers (McLaughlin, 2009). Apart from the obvious virtue of research being conceived and directed by experts in
their own situation and needs, other recommendations include the
capacity to transfer the power to define the reality of children in care
away from professionals towards the young people themselves, and
the advantages to individuals of participation in research activity, in
terms of skills acquired and confidence gained.

Another influence is the more general social trend away from the
notion of patients or clients as passive recipients of services from
experts, in favour of a more democratic view of service users as cus-
tomers or consumers, able to exercise choice and to harness services to
meet their own needs. This trend has been facilitated by access to the
internet and the information it yields, and the rise in the use of social
networking. Service users may also become professional researchers, influenced by the significance of their reflections on their own
experience. Well-known figures in the field of looked after children's

research include Zachari Duncalf, Jim Goddard, James Mallon and Peter McParlin.

Care leavers are also active in a range of other important ways in drawing attention to inadequate or abusive regimes in care settings, and in lobbying governments, arguing for policy change and leading service development activities. For more information about activities of care leavers see, for example, www.scottishthroughcare.org.uk and www.careleavers.com.

Summary

In this chapter we have been concerned to present the experience of residential care from the perspectives of children and young people themselves, through the use of case study examples and by high-lighting the importance of advocacy, the children's rights movement and service user research in raising awareness and campaigning to achieve improvements in care settings. For access to additional resources about this topic and others available online we recommend visiting the Library in the Sky, a superb resource hosted by the Northern Ireland advocacy organisation Voice of Young People in Care (VOYPIC), at www.libraryinthesky.org.

Thinking outside the box

Try to imagine the culture of a residential home, school or secure unit that values the perspectives and expertise of the young people who live there. As an observer, what characteristics might you notice? To assist your reflections on your own ideas, you might find it useful to read Ruth Emond's article in *Child and Youth Care Forum* in which she outlines proposals for a model that emphasises the power and functions of the resident group, rather than imposing adult notions of how young people should behave (Emond, 2004).

CHAPTER 4

Residential Care and Social Policy

Introduction

In this chapter we consider the broader social policy context within which residential care is provided in Scotland. The chapter begins by reviewing how decisions about placing children are made and how these have been influenced by trends or 'fashions' in responding to the needs of children who come into contact with the justice and child welfare systems. Current trends in Scotland are considered in the light of practice in other countries. The chapter then examines the concept of 'corporate parent' and the policy landscape that governs this idea.

Later in the chapter we introduce a range of special issues, including the controversial matter of 'safe holding' of children, the use of secure services, the development of specialist provision, leaving care and the education of children in residential care. The chapter ends by considering the different perspectives of child care experts, workers and young people.

Residential care or foster care

As outlined in Chapter 1, the decision-making process that leads to a child becoming looked after away from home begins with a referral to a children's hearing, at which a panel of three lay volunteers considers background reports and listens to the views of the child, family members and professionals. The children's hearing system is distinctive in that:

> it is the same tribunal, operating under the same procedural rules and having the same disposals available, that

deals with all children identified as being in need of help, for whatever reason (Norrie, 1997, p. 2).

This marks the Scottish system out as different to others within the UK. It is also unusual, and generally positively regarded, in an international sense, because it is strongly embedded in Scottish welfare and justice traditions so that it has resisted challenges, including those from the 'back to justice' movement concerned about the potential loss of civil rights in a system that emphasises the welfare needs of individual children (Hallett, 2000).

Referrals to the panel are received by an officer of the hearings' system, known as a 'reporter'. Reporters are typically professionally qualified and have practice experience in law, social work or in another specialist child care field. They are employed by the Scottish Children's Reporter Administration (SCRA; see www.scra.gov.uk), whose chief executive is also known as the Principal Reporter. Anyone can make a referral, though almost 90% of referrals are made by the police, even if at least some of these originated in concerns initially brought to the attention of police officers by members of the public. Despite this route of referral through the criminal justice system, in fact most referrals (86% in 2010/11) relate to what are termed 'care and protection' reasons. Even among those referred on offence grounds, around a third are also referred on care and protection grounds (SCRA, 2011a).

The children's hearings' system has its origins in the report of the Kilbrandon Committee, which met between 1961 and 1964 to consider the needs of 'children in trouble' (Asquith, 1995). Kilbrandon led to the Social Work (Scotland) Act 1968 and the hearings' system outlined in the Act was introduced in 1971. More recently the law governing the operation of hearings has been the Children (Scotland) Act 1995 and regulations dating from 1996, although a new statute has been introduced – the Children's Hearings (Scotland) Act 2011. Among the provisions in the new Act is one for a central administration, known as Children's Hearings Scotland, responsible for the recruitment, training and monitoring of children's panel members, and for national standards for the conduct of hearings (see www.chs.gov.uk).

Although the system has evolved in the four decades since its inception, the influence of Kilbrandon continues to underpin the operation of children's hearings today, notably the importance of the welfare of the child in determining action. The influence of Kilbrandon is maintained in the current statute, the Children (Scotland) Act 1995, and in time will undoubtedly mark replacement statutes. While there are several principles referring to the operation of panels (including the recruitment of lay volunteers and efforts to keep proceedings relatively informal and non-adversarial), three principles are regarded as of over-arching importance. The first of these is the view that in all court or hearing decisions the welfare of the child should be uppermost. The second is that the child has a right to be heard. Finally, often called the 'no order principle', the third principle refers to the view that no legal intervention should be made unless it is judged that to do so would be better for the child than making no order or supervision requirement at all.

An important function of the reporter is to investigate a referral and make a decision on the most appropriate approach to take. In only 14% of referral cases in 2010/11 was the outcome a decision to arrange a children's hearing (SCRA, 2011b). The rate of conversion of referrals to hearings was much higher in the past – around 52% in 1978 – and there has been a steady trend towards diverting children away from hearings (Hallett, 2000). Among the other disposals available to reporters are decisions to take no further action and voluntary measures agreed with the family or involving children's services.

The reporter arranges a hearing in circumstances where it seems likely that compulsory measures will be necessary. If the panel members subsequently decide these measures require a residential placement, the setting in which the child is placed depends on a number of factors, including the professional advice given to panel members, the availability of suitable provision and prevailing trends in relation to compulsory measures for children at risk. Professional advice prepared for the panel members to read prior to the hearing is contained in the initial enquiry report prepared by a social worker, taking account of the circumstances and judgements about the safety, well-being and needs of the child. Panel members also have access to reports prepared by specialists involved in assessing particular aspects of the child's circumstances, such as their education and mental health. The initial enquiry report may include a recommendation that the panel should consider foster care or residential care.

The panel makes a decision about the most appropriate placement, taking into account all the reports received and the views expressed at the hearing. If a residential placement is being considered, the panel may recommend a particular establishment, based on their judgement about its suitability for meeting the child's needs, though it is normally the responsibility of the local authority's chief social officer to make placement arrangements.

One of the key messages of the NRCCI was that while: 'integrated and holistic assessment is the key to identifying the needs of individual children … pressure within the system too often means that placement is resource-led rather than needs-led' (Hill, 2009, p. 51). Hill (2009) also argues that, while governments have repeated the rhetoric that residential care should be a positive choice, in reality there has been a tendency to prefer family placements. Two reasons are typically advanced for preferring foster placements: an assumption that family settings are always preferable to group care; and the relatively high cost of residential placements. In relation to cost, a report by Audit Scotland (2010) states that local authorities do not have the information they need to make the best use of resources and thus assumptions that alternatives to the apparently high cost of residential placements (e.g. supervision by a social worker, use of kinship or foster care) will be less expensive may in reality be wide of the mark.

While it is understandable that, for apparent economy and efficiency reasons, councils will seek to maximise the use of their own provision, this approach can lead to:

- decisions being made without all (and possibly the best) options for the child being considered;
- more decisions on independent placements being made in an emergency, when in-house provision cannot cope any longer with particularly challenging behaviour or specialist needs;
- unsuitable placements, which break down more often, resulting in more change and less stability for the child;

- the needs of the child not being effectively met (Audit Scotland, 2010, p. 24).

This approach might be characterised as using residential care as a last resort. One obvious danger in the approach is that there is an inevitability that services will become unviable and close down. This, in turn, means that there will be fewer options available to panels, and as the landscape of provision narrows the likelihood of matching children's needs to provision will decline. The NRCCI report proposes a number of situations when residential placement would be a positive choice, including when young people have had previous unsatisfactory experiences in family settings, when they display very challenging behaviour, when they have complex needs, or to keep siblings together (Hill, 2009).

An alternative to the last resort approach is a more strategic, managed approach, such as advocated by Audit Scotland (2010) and illustrated in a case study in their report. An obvious criticism of Audit Scotland's conclusions is that they are a statement of the obvious: few would not favour a more strategic approach, but in the face of budget pressures, a seemingly ever-changing landscape of providers and an increase in demand for sophisticated provision it remains a challenge to anticipate needs more than to react to crisis events:

> [The local authority] reviewed how it was managing children's residential care. The review was prompted by the council spending a lot more every year on these services and finding that it was purchasing more and more crisis places. The council revised its approach to commissioning services after assessing demand and expenditure. As a result of the review, the council:
>
> - forecast the demand for different types for services based on previous years' experience;
> - changed its decision-making structures to make quicker and better-informed decisions;
> - developed a specification for foster and residential services, both in-house and external;
> - evaluated current supplier arrangements in the context of the new specifications;

- investigated the market to establish what providers and services are available;
- met with potential suppliers to discuss the services required and budgetary constraints;
- undertook a tendering exercise and awarded contracts in late 2009 for two types of residential provision: crisis places, where a child's needs can be assessed before making decisions about the longer term; longer-term placements for children whose needs cannot be met in council residential units;
- estimated a budget based on the predicted demand and costs (Audit Scotland, 2010, p. 25).

The trend to favour family care settings over residential care was further reinforced by awareness of the 'historic' abuse experienced by children in some residential settings in Scotland, public knowledge of which only began to emerge during the 1980s. The reasons abusive cultures could emerge included not only an inadequate regulatory framework, poor monitoring of services and a largely untrained workforce, but also attitudes towards children that tolerated corporal punishment, inconsistencies in caring and a lack of acknowledgement in law of children's rights (Shaw, 2007).

It is important to point out that abuse of children happens in family settings too, including those where children have been placed for their safety. But residential care has attracted more criticism, perhaps because institutions that often exist anonymously in the community become more visible when things go wrong. The ideological preference for family care may occur because that is the more familiar setting for most people, at least in Scotland, including professionals. Foster care seems desirable, natural and normal, while residential care seems undesirable, formal and institutional (White, 2008). To counter this duality, White proposes a radical reframing of child care:

> With reframing there would no longer be the two-tier system, but a continuum or range of settings. Each would be encouraged to become what it can best be for the good of children. Therapeutic communities might be home for some of their children; there might be foster relationships

within them. Large foster households would become the residential communities of the future. And there is some small glimmer of hope that the throttling industrial service model will be held at bay, as the personal, private and family aspects of a child's life are re-emphasised (White, 2008).

Residential care in Scotland compared with other countries

As seen in Chapter 1, about 10% of looked after children in Scotland lives in residential care, though the proportion rises to 20% among 12–15 year olds. We also noted that the proportion was much higher in the past – 36%, for example, in 1976. In fact there has been a general trend in the developed countries away from large-scale, institutional provision to a combination of smaller, residential provision, and to foster care and community services (Kendrick, 2010). Nevertheless, as Kendrick's briefing note for the Scottish Government also mentions, the balance of residential care to foster care varies between countries. In Japan, for example, little use is made of foster care, while in Germany and Denmark the balance between residential care and foster care is roughly even. The proportions are low – between 10% and 20% – in many countries, such as Scotland, England, Ireland, USA, Norway and Sweden. Even within countries there can be wide regional variations. Australia is an example of a country with a very low proportion of looked after children in residential care, at 5%. In this context it is interesting to note that such has been the lack of residential options in Australia that many children are also 'cared for' in hostels for the homeless and other provision run by the housing department of each state (Ainsworth and Hansen, 2011). The lack of options has, however, led to calls for new residential provision (Liddell *et al.*, 2006), and there have been a number of new initiatives including residential services for Aboriginal children and families in Queensland (Downey *et al.*, 2011).

Institutional-based child care is more common in the developing countries. The reasons for this include the greater prevalence of orphaned children as a result of disease such as HIV/AIDS, famine and wars, and also where children are abandoned as a result of family poverty or disability. In some countries foster care options are relatively uncommon or unknown. The use of institutional care in such circumstances has raised concerns among international monitoring agencies, such as UNICEF, chiefly because of the tendency to accommodate large numbers of children in desperately poor conditions, staffed by inadequately trained workers who often fail to provide individual attention. For example, one report on child care reforms in54 central and eastern Europe and the former Soviet Union highlighted the adverse effects on children of being raised in bad institutional care. These included poor health, physical underdevelopment, hearing and vision problems, motor skill delays, reduced cognitive and social ability and abuse by staff (Carter, 2005).

Another concern is the use of institutional care for very young children who:

> rarely have the opportunity to form an attachment to a parent figure/carer, and they spend less time on play, social interaction, and individual care than children in a family. Thus, the institutional care of children less than three years old may have negative effects on neural functioning at this crucial period of brain development (Browne *et al.*, 2006, pp. 485–6).

While these inadequacies are mainly a function of large, impersonal institutions, they serve as a potent reminder that small residential units and foster care options in themselves do not provide the necessary conditions for normal child development. The testimony of children who have experienced multiple placements is witness to that.

The corporate parent and the policy landscape

The term 'corporate parent' is now in widespread use throughout the UK, connoting the idea that representatives of the state should act towards looked after children as they would towards their own children. This is how the foreword to the Scottish government's policy document, *These Are Our Bairns*, introduced the concept of central and local government behaving like a parent:

> Like any good parent, we want our children to enjoy school and do well there; we want them to be healthy and happy, secure and confident. We want them to go on to college or

university, to find good jobs, to have loving relationships and happy lives. In addition, we want them to be included and effective members of our communities, indeed in the fullness of time to be good parents themselves ... Being a good corporate parent is more than fulfilling your statutory duties. Over the years, despite good intentions and invest-ment, we have collectively failed the children and young people who have been entrusted to us. We have a social and moral obligation to do our very best for those most vulner-able members of our communities and to show that we can and will do better as corporate parents (Scottish Govern-ment, 2008b, p. v).

The idea is that the 'social and moral obligations' should be owned by individual teachers, social workers, carers, school nurses and other professionals who have opportunities to support, influence and encourage looked after children. *These Are Our Bairns* sets out the responsibilities pertaining to staff in particular services. For exam-ple, one of the tasks specified for social work services is:

Make sure that all the child or young person's achievements are recognised and the ones most important to the young person are remembered and recorded (Scottish Govern-ment, 2008b, p. 33).

This particular requirement is interesting in itself, since a common criticism of social work recording is the tendency to note in detail assessments, which invariably feature deficits, and incidents involving children that worry staff. The fact that the statement refers to the indi-vidual child, rather than to looked after children collectively, is reveal-ing since it turns on its head the common managerial requirement to focus on 'policy outcomes' (such as targets achieved or missed) in favour of 'developmental outcomes', which record regular achieve-ments – the 'outcomes that matter' (Fulcher and Garfat, 2012).

While policymakers and politicians are clearly convinced of the value of corporate parenting, principally because it is consistent with the desire to facilitate integrated children's services and joined-up working, others are more sceptical. Some of this scepticism relates to the limited capacity of local authorities to provide the full range of supports typically given by families: for example, in using contacts to find employment. While there are examples of councils providing training posts for care leavers and champions' schemes, whereby council officers mentor looked after children, these are not widespread. Other critics regard the concept as 'an unwelcome extension of the reach of the state into family life, downgrading the role of birth parent to just another partner in the business of rearing their child', with the implication that 'parenting is too important and too difficult a job to be left to parents alone' (Clements, 2007).

Special issues

In this section of the chapter we outline briefly a small number of special issues that have attracted the attention of policymakers. These are the use of physical restraint ('safe holding') with children in residential care, the provision of secure services, the development of specialist provision, the education of children in residential care, the health of children in residential care and leaving care.

Safe holding

The context for this area of policy in relation to residential care is the acknowledgement that children who have experienced inconsistent parenting or abuse may on occasions behave in ways that are physically threatening to staff and other young people, and which may also put themselves at risk of physical injury or even death. Although there is no clear definition of physical restraint in Scottish child care legislation, the justification for its use lies in the common law duty of care for children and more particularly the local authority's duty under the Children (Scotland) Act 1995 to safeguard children in care, and there is very detailed guidance for intervening safely (Davidson *et al.*, 2005). The guidance, known as *Holding Safely,* makes clear that workers need to be given appropriate training and that they should restrain in ways that maintain the child's dignity and right not to be harmed. The guidance also points out that the practice of restraining children cannot be divorced from broader concerns about the quality of relationships between workers and children and the ethos of the residential setting. Writing about lessons to be learned following an inquiry into widespread abuse of children by staff of a residential school in Scotland, Davidson highlights the importance of the development of a strong, positive staff culture and the capacity to recruit and retain competent, confident residential workers (Davidson, 2010).

It is somewhat ironic that the use of restraint coexists alongside a degree of confusion about appropriate physical contact between adults and children in residential settings, including, for example, giving hugs and the use of touch and proximity for the everyday purposes of reassurance and comforting distressed children. The inconsistency in practice, which such ambivalence produces, was perceptively observed by a young person who told one of the authors that staff where he lived said they could not put sun screen on him but 'they can hold you down'. This was not said with anger, or even annoyance, but with recognition of the illogical behaviour.

Some commentators argue for a zero tolerance approach, which would never countenance physical restraint, but most workers believe that this is simply not realistic. The problem is that it is easier to fulfil the technical aspects of restraint – learning how to hold safely, completing the essential paperwork, notifying parents and social workers – than to cope with the more complex ethical dimensions. In order to be confident about dealing with the ambiguities of relationships with young people who have experienced very damaging life events, residential workers need to be able to call on significant reserves of skill and understanding. The best residential settings 'have the potential to reduce and possibly eliminate the need for physical restraint; they can also make experiences of therapeutic containment possible, of which physical restraint may simply be a small part' (Steckley, 2010).

Secure services
Secure care settings exist to make provision for young people who present a serious risk to themselves or to others. These will include young people under eighteen who have problematic alcohol and drug use or other self-harming behaviours that staff in other settings have found difficult or impossible to manage. They also provide safe care for young people under sixteen who have been convicted of very serious offences. In fact, a relatively small number of young people are looked after in secure settings – an average of eighty-five during

2010/11 (Scottish Government, 2012b). According to official statistics, this is a larger number than in Finland, which may be an underestimate, and a smaller number than in Sweden – both countries of similar population size to Scotland.

The Scottish government has advanced the following five principles in relation to the provision of secure care, indicating the commitment both to reduce the need for such facilities and also to maintain an appropriate range of provision:

- our ultimate ambition must be to have no child in Scotland in secure care and we must actively work to reduce the need for secure care;
- every child in Scotland should get the best start in life and the right help when they need it in order to prevent risks turning into poor outcomes;
- where it is possible to meet the needs of high-risk young people safely and cost-effectively in their communities, then these opportunities should be maximised;
- for the very small number of children whose needs can only be met in secure care, then we have to provide a high-quality and nurturing environment that addresses their needs;
- a placement in secure care must be part of a planned journey through the care system (Scottish Government, 2009).

This commitment recognises two factors. First, there is the acknowledgement that providing secure care is essentially a euphemism for locking up children, a practice that most people, including staff working in the centres, find uncomfortable. Secondly, is the recognition that the children who end up in secure settings have essentially been failed by the society that brought them up.

Secure care is often characterised as opposing principles: children need to be kept securely in their best interests; or children are locked up and deprived of liberty as if they were in prison. From a Finnish perspective this duality is naïve, and they prefer the term 'closed accommodation'. This presents secure care as similar to closed mental health provision, which has general public acceptance. This acceptability occurs because secure care exists within a child welfare perspective, but the disadvantage is that, because the best interests of children are defined by adults, children's rights are less prominent and this in turn makes for a low level of scrutiny (Pösö *et al.*, 2010).

Disability services
Within the residential sector in Scotland there has traditionally been provision for children with disabilities. In 2009 there were thirteen residential schools, eight care homes and thirty-six short-break facilities, most provided by the voluntary sector (Hill, 2009). Not all children in these facilities are looked after, though children with disabilities are more likely to be in residential settings than their non-disabled peers. As a consequence of a combination of more inclusive attitudes to disability and legislation such as the Standards in Scottish Schools etc. Act 2000, which introduced the presumption that all children should normally be educated in mainstream schools, the number of residential places in schools exclusively for children with disabilities has reduced during the past decade. There has been a parallel trend for special residential schools to focus on children with multiple and complex needs and for a growth in short-break provision.

Among the policy considerations that are raised by these trends is the need for a broader range of options, including community-based services to support families looking after disabled children at home, the need for more foster and adoptive parents who are confident in their capacity to care for children with complex needs, and residential settings that are regarded as placements of choice rather than of last resort (Stalker, 2008).

The education of children in residential care
There are different contexts in which children in residential care attend school: one is where care and education are provided by the same agency and often on the same site, as in the case of residential schools and secure care settings; another is where children living in group homes in the community attend local schools. There is a third context, whereby children live with their families, or with foster carers, and attend a residential school as 'day pupils'. This option is used in situations in which a child's education would be

disrupted by a return to a mainstream school (e.g. in close proximity to national examinations), as a way of easing the transition out of residential care (i.e. by not making a change of school at the same time as the change of placement), and where a child living in the community needs a more closely structured form of schooling or access to additional supports only available in the residential school.

In recent years there has been a particular focus on the education of looked after children. The generally poor academic performance of looked after children at school has 'become something of a litmus test of the perceived inefficiency of children's social services as a whole' (Berridge *et al.*, 2008, p. 14). The policy context is outlined in the *Looked After Children and Young People: We Can and Must do Better* report (Scottish Executive, 2007). This document highlights the need to improve the educational outcomes of looked after children who tend to have:

- lower than average attendance at school;
- lower than average attainment;
- a greater risk of being excluded from school;
- more frequent changes of school;
- part-time education;
- less likelihood of being in positive destinations (i.e. education, training or employment) after leaving school (Scottish Executive, 2007).

It appears that children in residential care have significantly lower average school attendance than children in foster care; the latter group in fact attend, on average, as well as or better than non-looked after children (Scottish Government, 2011).

Although there have been improvements in attendance and attainment in recent years, the gap between looked after children and their non-looked after peers has not narrowed, and this is a matter of concern to politicians. In the autumn of 2011 the Education and Culture Committee of the Scottish Parliament began an inquiry into the problem. The Members of the Scottish Parliament (MSPs) identified several themes where coherent practice responses are needed, including:

- readiness to learn which would result, in part, from feeling safe in school and knowing that bullying by peers was being addressed;

- support at school, co-ordinated by a 'designated manager' and capable of addressing both gaps in education and encouraging special aptitudes;
- effective joint working, through good communication and sharing of information between agencies (Scottish Parliament, 2012).

The factors in relation to education are complex and there is no space to address these adequately in this book. Readers interested in exploring the topic in more detail should refer to the CELCIS website (www.celcis.org), where reports are archived and news items routinely posted, and several journals have devoted special issues to the matter: for example, *Adoption and Fostering*, Vol. 31, No. 1 (2007); *Scottish Journal of Residential Child Care*, Vol. 7, No. 1 (2008); *Children and Youth Services Review*, Vol. 34, No. 6 (2012); *European Journal of Social Work*, Vol. 16, No. 10 (2013).

Before leaving this section, it is important to emphasise the role of children's services professionals, particularly teachers, in encouraging looked after children in their education. Professionals tend to work with children during short periods of their lives – in the case of secondary teachers this 'window' is between eleven and seventeen – and so they do not often get to see how children develop as adults. There is a danger they make assumptions based on stereotypes.

This point was made powerfully by two young students, describing their experiences to a conference organised by Buttle UK, a charity that administers a quality mark for further and higher education institutions providing additional support arrangements for students from a looked after background (www.buttleuk.org). One student recounted that, when she told a teacher of her interest in applying to university, the response, delivered sympathetically, was: 'I don't know how to tell you this, but people like you don't go to university.' Another student had a very different experience when a teacher said: 'Why don't you become a lawyer?'

The authors are very aware that our own efforts to draw attention to the typically poor educational outcomes of children from care *at school* risk stigmatising looked after children as a group. We know that many adults from care backgrounds have more circuitous routes into education, particularly involving attendance at a further education college, and many have become high achievers as a result (Duncalf, 2010).

The health of children in residential care

Research evidence suggests that looked after children are likely to experience a far higher incidence of health problems than young people in the general population. The reasons for a child or young person being in care are often those also associated with poor health, such as the effects of poverty, chaotic lifestyles, substance misuse, neglect or abuse. For example, one study of children aged 5–15 who remained in care for at least a year found that 72% had an emotional or behavioural problem at the point of being received into care (Sempik *et al.*, 2008), while another found that 86% of children in residential care surveyed had incomplete childhood health screening and 71% had not achieved full immunisation status (Residential Health Care Project Team, 2004).

Scottish young people in general appear to have poorer health outcomes than young people elsewhere in the UK, and this difference is likely to be mirrored in the looked after population. For example, one survey found that 'accommodated' children (i.e. those in residential and foster care) aged 11–17 in Scotland were twice as likely to smoke, drink alcohol or take drugs as their counterparts in England (Meltzer *et al.*, 2004). The high frequency of moves among looked after children means there is a heightened risk of missing out on routine medical, dental, hearing and eyesight checks.

The Scottish government's policy document *These Are Our Bairns* reminds local authorities, health boards and related agencies of their corporate parenting duties to promote health, to identify health-related risks and to treat health problems (Scottish Government, 2008b). More specifically, NHS health boards in Scotland received advice about their responsibilities towards looked after children by means of 'CEL 16', a memorandum to chief executives of health boards. CEL 16 included the recommendation that each health board should nominate a board director to take corporate responsibility for looked after children and care leavers, and that:

> The director will ensure that for every looked after child or young person who has general and mental health needs

assessed as part of their health assessment, the person undertaking that health assessment takes responsibility for ensuring their care plan is delivered/co-ordinated as appropriate (Healthcare Policy and Strategy Directorate, 2009).

Concern has been expressed about difficulties that young people with mental health problems have in accessing child and adolescent mental health services (CAMHS). For example, the Scottish government has set a target that by March 2013 no one will wait more than twenty-six weeks from referral to treatment, reducing to eighteen weeks by 2014. Barnardo's, among other organisations, argues that, while this would be an improvement, even a wait of this length is too long for children with severe mental health difficulties. The charity also says that services are 'patchy and inconsistent' across Scotland (Barnardo's Scotland, 2012).

On the positive side, children in residential care should have access to looked after children's nurses, who provide clinical services and advocate for greater awareness of the health needs of looked after children. A network of specialist nurses has produced a directory of services and a framework to guide practice (LAAC Scottish Nurse Forum, 2008; NHS Education for Scotland, 2008).

Leaving care
An influential report by Scotland's Commissioner for Children and Young People (2008), *Sweet 16?*, highlights the fact that, while law and government policy give a strong emphasis on helping young people to stay in care until age eighteen, in fact eight times as many people leave care at age sixteen as at eighteen. The report points out that young people are entitled to aftercare services only if they had been looked after by the local authority on or after reaching the minimum school leaving age of sixteen. The commissioner's research shows that some young people were discharged from supervision requirements shortly before reaching this threshold, thus making them ineligible for aftercare support, even though they may have spent a substantial or significant part of their life in care.

In fact, eligibility for care leaver support services, such as the vacation grant available to care leavers on higher education courses, is a very complex area, and one that lies in the interface between devolved (i.e. Scottish government) and reserved (i.e. Westminster government) powers. This is because social work and education services are devolved, but the social security (benefits) system is reserved. Even agencies that receive direct funding from the Scottish government (e.g. the Student Awards Agency Scotland) use eligibility criteria based on UK-wide benefit rules.

Leaving care is not solely a matter for young people aged 16–18, but refers to the experience of children and young people changing placements and transitioning out of care. The work of NRCCI indicates that 'the important progress that young people make during their period in residential care is not always sustained after they leave (Hill, 2009, p. 25).

The perspectives of experts, workers and young people

Although policy is the vehicle for systematising the concerns of a range of stakeholders – including the public, politicians and academics – and translating these into legislation and formal guidance for improving services, we end this chapter by acknowledging that there is no guarantee that the changes that result actually make life better for those most closely affected. The most commonly articulated perspectives are those of the 'experts', often academics, such as the writers of this book, whose reflections are affected by their status as outside observers, even if their academic work has its roots in practice experience. There is an important place for the research skills of the academic, the policymaker's knowledge of broader issues and the politician's passion for making a difference

Inevitably, though, these professional perspectives suffer from the very detachment that is valued in these disciplines, and for that reason we can learn a great deal from the impact of hearing or reading more personal accounts of residential care. We quote two such stories here. The first is by a retired worker of many years' experience, while the second was written by a young adult reflecting on her own experience of growing up in residential care.

The worker's account

It is hard not to be pessimistic about the future of residential child care. The housemothers in the 1960s felt that they did a good job and felt valued. Many residential child care workers I meet feel fearful, de-skilled, hopeless and worthless. What a message to give to the children in their care. The service seems driven by policies and procedures that have very little to do with the day-to-day life of children. The risk-aversion culture with everybody watching their back for fear of contravening the health and safety and child protection procedures, or not keeping the all-important paperwork up to date, prevents spontaneity and many of the 'messy bits', which are the essence of healthy relationships. Residential care continues to be a last resort, despite claims to the contrary. Therefore many children are so emotionally damaged by the time they come into care they need specialist help, which is not available as it is seen as too expensive (Cross, 2011).

The care leaver's account

Residential care is the only option for some children because foster care, which essentially mirrors a family unit, is often too frightening and painful for a child who has left a dysfunctional family. Residential care is so important, and should be an equal option for children alongside fostering, because it has more boundaries and rules and regulations, which many young people might find annoying but do respond to, and the staff are carers rather than parents. Often children are placed in foster care because it is a cheaper option, but for many children it doesn't work because of the fear of being in a family unit, and some children can end up going through up to fifty foster carers. At the same time, some care homes are just too big, with large numbers of disturbed children living together under one roof, which generates its own problems. When I first went into care, it was to a large council-run home, which housed up to fifteen children at any one time. The place was utter chaos and I learned things there that I would have been better off not knowing – how to smoke drugs, how to be a good shoplifter and how to run away. So a key point about effective residential care is getting the balance right by reducing the number of children living together. Instead of demolishing residential care, we need to change it by creating smaller units. I could not be managed in such a large care home, primarily due to mental health and safety issues stemming from my difficult background. I needed a residential setting with fewer children and a more personalised care plan. My next placement went some way towards that. The organisation that I was placed in aimed to have as few children living together as possible, and during my placement I only lived with one other youngster, in a regular house on a regular street. A young person was placed in rented accommodation in the community and that would be their home, a manager would oversee the running of that 'unit', and there would be three staff working on a rota system covering the entire week, twenty-four hours a day. There was a structured system of education, therapy leisure activities. The placement was by no means perfect, and in my first nine months I went through more than ten carers, but I eventually found the right one. She was a teacher, a mother herself, someone who had travelled the world and, most important, someone who was going to put meals on the table, encourage me back into education and broaden my world view. This isn't that different from what you would hope to gain from foster care; however, it worked for me because my carer wasn't trying to be my mother but she looked after me, and that is what all children need (Howley, 2011).

Summary

This chapter has presented an account of the policy context within which residential care is provided in Scotland. The chapter outlined the policy landscape through several specific issues and examined in particular the concept of the local authority and its partners as corporate parents. We end by inviting you to consider the characteristics of quality residential care.

Thinking outside the box

What do you consider to be the key factors required to ensure that residential care is more widely regarded as a positive choice, and is valued by children, families, social workers and the wider public, rather than a place of last resort?

CHAPTER 5

The Purpose and Function of Residential Child Care

Introduction

In this chapter we address the question of the purpose of residential placement, and the place of residential homes and schools in the spectrum of social services. We show how official thinking about the purpose of residential care has developed in recent years, and chart the emergence of 'statements of functions and objectives'. We also note the contrast between these government policy aspirations and the reality at local authority level, where the preference for family placement and overall shortage of placements impacts on the actual use of residential care. Despite the ideal of moving children on a planned basis, in reality a lot of moves happen on an emergency basis and some placements in residential care are for very short periods, essentially holding a child until a longer-term placement can be found. As noted in Chapter 1, the residential sector is diverse, and in this chapter we describe the various types of residential care and how they are categorised.

The inter-relationship between residential and foster and kinship care placements

Residential placement is very often intended to be short-term or temporary while a longer-term family placement is identified. It is, however, accepted by social workers and children's panel members that residential placement on a longer-term basis is needed for some children who have expressed a clear desire not to be fostered and also for some children whose behaviour is so challenging that foster placement is not normally considered. So typically children will be admitted to residential care in a family crisis and then returned home to their parents after a few days, weeks or months, when the family situation has stabilised sufficiently; or they will be placed in a residential unit longer-term after previous placements have broken down. In some cases the 'return home' breaks down and the child will be returned to residential care. A child may also be admitted to residential care after a foster placement has broken down. Generally speaking, the younger the child the shorter is the stay in a residential home pending a move to a foster placement.

In summary, residential placement has become mainly a placement for children aged twelve and above, and in most local authority children's homes there will be a mixture of children on short- and long-term placements, the latter providing for children who cannot be returned to the family home and for whom a foster placement is unsuitable or unavailable. The *Matching Resources to Needs* report published as part of NRCCI includes the following in its summary of the young people found in residential care:

- most children in residential care are aged 12–15;
- over the last fifteen years, there has been a growth in the numbers of children aged under twelve looked after in residential care, often for very short periods;
- a significant minority of young people in residential care were formerly in foster care or other residential placements, some with repeated placement breakdowns (Hill, 2009, p. 5).

There have been varied efforts to address the matter of repeated placement breakdown of young children in foster care. One leading voluntary-sector residential provider, Sycamore Services (part of the Aberlour agency), set up a special residential unit for severely traumatised children aged 5–10. Sycamore responded to an increase in referrals of children regarded as being too young for the provision in their therapeutic units by encouraging their workers to use concepts derived from attachment theory and their understanding of trauma to work therapeutically with the children to provide stability and prepare them for long-term fostering or residential care or in a few cases a return to the parental home (Elsley, 2009).

Statements of function

In order to make care more purposeful and to prevent children 'drifting', the idea that children's homes should have a written statement of functions and objectives was promoted. This concept had been articulated during the 1980s and became a statutory requirement via the *Residential Regulations 1987* (Great Britain, 1987). The idea was strongly endorsed in *Another Kind of Home*:

> It is imperative that each home should be clear about its own functions and objectives ... [These] are bound to be reviewed from time to time, to reflect changes in needs, policies and professional practice (Skinner, 1992).

But research into the use of the statements had also revealed that their quality was highly variable and, 'on the whole the statements of functions and objectives are not being used as effective tools in the management of residential child care' (Skinner, 1992, pp. 17–18).

The reasons for having a written statement were that it should help staff identify the purpose of the home and promote consistent practice. It was intended as a safeguard to prevent children being placed just because a bed was available. It was also part of an aspiration that social work intervention should be planned and purposeful, and that children's placement should be carefully monitored and regularly reviewed so that their needs and rights were met. A statement of function and objectives would set out whether the home was intended for short- or longer-term placement and whether perhaps it also filled an emergency or respite function through having one or more places/beds identified for that purpose. Statements would typically specify the target age group and whether the main purpose was to rehabilitate children to parental homes, provide 'treatment' for emotional or behavioural problems, prepare them for fostering/adoption or, in the case of older children not returning home, to provide preparation for independent living.

The importance of a children's home having a clear purpose and philosophy of care was reinforced in research studies that appeared to support the claim that a good home is:

> a small home run by somebody who has a clear idea about what the home is trying to achieve and how to do it and

which encourages contact with family members while respecting the fact that many children do not want to live at home (DOH, 1998, p. 44).

Services for children with disabilities

The purpose or function of residential services for children with disabilities stands in some contrast to the non-disability sector and is much less subject to fundamental questioning. Residential forms of care for children with disabilities are generally of three main kinds:

- respite services, increasingly referred to as 'short-break' services;
- longer-term homes;
- residential schools for children with complex and multiple disabilities.

The first group of homes is by far the most numerous, and there are very few homes in the second category. The third group also has few homes but tends to have long histories of serving particular groups of children, such as those attending the Royal Blind School.

Respite, or short-break, services

This group of services had expanded greatly since the development of community care and the closure of long-stay hospitals for people with disabilities, which had included some wards for children. Today services tend to be provided at the family home, so that the family unit can be maintained. Families with children who have disabilities are entitled to additional cash benefits and services such as transport to schools. Where there are particular strains on families or the demands of day-to-day care are very high, children and families may also get access to short breaks. Children may spend periods of time in residential respite services at a weekend, or for a few days during the week, or during school holidays. Such short breaks are now normally provided in small homes for between four and eight children. These are usually run by voluntary organisations, such as Action for Children or Quarrier's. The term 'short break' was proposed in a major report into disability services, *The Same As You?* (Scottish Executive, 2000). The report's authors urge the change in terminology to encourage services to focus on creating positive experiences for the child, rather than only on giving parents respite from the demands of care.

Longer-term care

Despite the commitment to supporting children in their family home, there are some disabled children who receive long-term residential care because their families are unable to look after them. There are also some children with complex health problems, which may be life-limiting. Some of these young people live with parents and receive intensive medical support on a domiciliary basis, but there are a few who receive this level of care in a long-term foster care or residential disability service.

Disabled children and 'looked after' status

The key thing to note about the purpose of residential care in the disability sector is that the children are usually not seen as being 'in care' in the same sense as children who are receiving compulsory supervision. The parents of disabled children do not usually feel distressed about their children being in residential care, and rather they may be pleased that the children can get a few days in a residential unit at regular intervals. There is much less stigma attached to these kinds of services, because the placement does not replace the children's home life, and there is no sense that the child has been neglected or abused.

Compared to long-term care in a special hospital or other more institutionalised type of care, contemporary provision is less problematic, at least at the level of basic purpose and role. Nevertheless, any child who is looked after away from home for more than twenty-four hours at a time is defined as 'looked after' under the terms of the Children (Scotland) Act 1995. This does not include private arrangements whereby parents agree that their child should go to live with friends or other family members. The annual 'looked after children' statistical returns made by local authorities categorise respite care for children with disabilities under the heading 'planned series of short-term placements'. Around 1,200 children and young people under the age of twenty-one receive this kind of care in a residential unit, and a further 900 or so in foster care placements (Scottish Government, 2012b).

Matching needs and resources: Identifying functions of residential care

Having considered the purposes of residential placement for children with complex disabilities we now return to examine the purpose of residential placement for children who have been placed through a supervision requirement issued at a children's hearing or on a voluntary basis by agreement between the parents and social work services.

In Skinner's (1992) review of residential child care part of the defence of the residential option lay in accepting certain constraints on its use. Following the influence of John Bowlby and other writers on attachment, and the importance placed on early attachment to a primary carer, Skinner (1992) took the view that residential care was especially unsuitable for younger children. This influenced the guidance issued with the Children (Scotland) Act 1995, which stated that a child under twelve should be placed in residential care 'only exceptionally' (Scottish Office, 1997, p. 70). It was recognised by local authorities that if large sibling groups needed to be accommodated then exceptions to the policy could be made by keeping the siblings together in a children's home. Thus residential care became predominantly a 'teenage' service.

The desire to keep younger children in families was facilitated by the facts that the expanding group of foster carers was generally more enthusiastic about taking younger children and that placement breakdown of teenagers in foster care was common. Skinner (1992) went far beyond a simple age demarcation in trying to define what residential care should be for. His review lists a number of groups of young people for whom residential care was to be considered a 'positive choice'. Under the heading 'appropriate and inappropriate use' the following groups of young people, aged over twelve, were identified for residential placement:

- those who need emergency care, including perhaps some who need short–term care and family work to support family rehabilitation;
- long-term care where the need for long-term care had not been identified until the child was in their teens, or where family placement had repeatedly broken down;

- young people with needs for additional specialist therapeutic or educational services;
- complex needs but short-term care;
- keeping sibling groups together – although the report added the interesting and unrealised suggestion that 'the alternative of staff moving into the family home should generally be preferred' (Skinner, 1992).

The NRCCI (Hill, 2009) attempted to define those young people for whom a residential placement might be the best option. By this time the continuing presence of a few younger children in residential care, and the existence of very seriously traumatised younger children who had not been able to be contained within foster homes, led to different conclusions. The NRCCI made the following suggestions about the use or function of residential placement:

- residential care should be used to avoid repeated foster-breakdown; the group had noted the problem of multiple placement breakdowns and said that a residential placement must be considered sooner;
- for children with serious attachment-based behaviour problems and/or who are a serious risk to the community;
- the committee members explicitly rejected Skinner's 'no under-twelves' formulation, making the case for a small number of younger children with severe attachment difficulties, related to highly neglectful or abusive parenting, to be considered for residential care;
- they also said that for some children making an earlier decision that they should enter residential care would lead to better outcomes (Hill, 2009).

Emergency care
Acting as an emergency resource or safety net for other parts of the care system is not usually presented as a positive purpose for residential care, but in practice it is a major feature of current use. Skinner's (1992) report had identified 'emergency care' as one appropriate use of residential care but that had been in the context of a child being removed from their family on an emergency basis. In recent years, however, planned placements into local authority residential care

have become rare, and residential care is acting as a resource for a wider system where removal from home or failing foster placement routinely happens on an emergency rather than planned basis. This suggests that the social workers supporting children at home are under enormous pressures to keep children within families, where there are major stresses, and similarly that the foster care system is being burdened with expectations it cannot meet.

High levels of emergency admissions and the frequency of placement breakdowns suggest the system as a whole is somewhat dysfunctional. In practice, local authority residential care functions as a fall-back for the fostering and adoption system; when such placements break down children are accommodated in residential care (McPheat *et al.*, 2007). Similarly, the voluntary and private sector residential schools and 'crisis services' act as emergency resources when children in foster care or local authority residential care experience severe behavioural crises and cannot be contained in their units or foster placements.

Close support units and 'crisis services'
Currently, many local authority units are described as 'generic' in their function, in that they attempt to meet a range of individual needs, and the main differentiation of function is between short- and longer-term units (Hill, 2009). Some organisations, in local authorities and the independent sector, have developed units that are described as 'intensive' or 'close support' units. The development of these units – which are usually differentiated from mainstream ones by a higher staff ratio and 'tighter' admissions criteria – is closely associated with the search for alternatives to secure care. The aim of such provision is to meet the needs of very vulnerable or volatile young people who may be at risk of being placed in secure care.

A number of reports into the need for secure care places in the 1990s had identified pressure on the system and an apparent shortage of places. The recommendations made in these reports suggested that what was needed was not more secure places but rather more forms of intensive support where children could be closely supervised and their behaviour 'treated' or 'addressed', but without the need for locked conditions (SWSIS, 1996; 1999). 'Close support' units have also been developed on the same campus of some secure units, where they function as a planned, 'step-down' option, for some of the children who have been placed temporarily in secure care as a means of gradually reintroducing them to open residential conditions.

A number of private providers have also sought to meet the need for alternatives to secure accommodation by providing a form of service sometime described as a 'crisis service'. We have explained that many residential units take children on an emergency basis, but some units have found a niche by taking children who are regarded as difficult to support and whose placements in all other types of provision have broken down. One characteristic of some of these services is that they are singleton placements, where one child is looked after by a team of staff on a shift basis. Critics of this type of provision point out that the young person is isolated from anything resembling a family-type environment and normal social contact with other young people. An alternative perspective is, however, that these placements can be acceptable as they should only last a matter of weeks to provide close supervision to young people in serious danger. They might be considered appropriate, for example, for young people with a history of repeated attempts at suicide or severe risk-taking behaviours, and the placements can provide them with a route to stability and preparation for a more conventional setting.

Shared care
It has been argued (Elsley, 2006; Hill, 2009) that more use could be made of long-term 'shared care' approaches to residential placement, where a child spends part of a week with their parents or other family members and part of the week in a children's home: for example, the child might stay in the children's home during the school week and in the family home at weekends and during holidays. This type of care approximates to forms of 'shared care', which are common in the disability sector, whereby children receive regular periods of respite with a foster carer or residential service because the family finds it impossible to provide full-time care. Such shared care as does exist in the non-disability sector tends to be short-term, while a child is in the process of being rehabilitated to parents, and where the aim is to end the residential placement. Longer-term shared care could give

some children stability and preserve a good level of family connection in situations in which the parents do not have the capacity solely to look after the child. Usually this is seen as costly, as each child has to have their own bedroom, and thus from a local authority's point of view a bed that is unoccupied for part of a week is a waste of a scarce resource. There are, however, interesting new developments in some local authorities, which combine outreach intensive family support from residential child care workers with planned short-break care for some young people in a dedicated respite resource. The difficulties experienced by most local authorities in providing this kind of option could be viewed as an unintended consequence of reducing numbers and units, and losing flexibility in the process.

Summary
This chapter has described the development of policy about the proper uses of residential care. It has also noted the different types of residential provision that have developed in the local authority, charitable and private sectors. Attention has been drawn to the statutory requirement for each home to have a regularly reviewed statement of function and objectives. While most local authorities retain their own children's homes and continue to invest in them (as we saw in Chapter 2) they have continued to reduce places overall. In a context in which more children are coming into the wider care system this tends to result in homes becoming highly pressured environments, which contain some very 'troubled' and 'troublesome' children, with some children passing through for very short placements. Furthermore, as noted in Chapter 4, such is the shortage of places that there is also pressure to move children on at sixteen or seventeen despite the lack of supportive services for young people at this stage.

The desire to have a clear set of aims and functions is invaluable. However, until there is adequate provision – including some 'empty beds' to facilitate real choice and a greater degree of differentiation of functions – residential care is likely to continue to be mainly a residual and 'safety net' type of service and will not properly realise its potential.

Thinking outside the box

We are familiar with the idea of 'assessing' children's needs, but Leon Fulcher argues that before placing a child a social worker should also assess the residential facility to make sure it is well suited to a child's needs. He proposes '12 variables' by which residential services could be assessed (Fulcher, 2001). Imagine that you are a social worker, or perhaps a children's panel member, and have to make a decision about a child who is in need of education and care. How would you decide which one to recommend? What criteria might you develop to help make such a decision?

To help you with this task we provide some details below about two quite different residential schools.

Kibble Education and Care Centre (www.kibble.org) is a charitable trust in continuous use since its foundation in 1859 in Paisley. It provides residential and day places for approximately 120 young people aged twelve plus, in residential houses of between four and eight youngsters. The centre has its own psychological services, the Specialist Interventions Services team, which provides a range of specialist assessments and interventions for young people and their families. Kibble has also developed a wide range of services beyond its core residential provision. These include the extensive Kibble Works programme of skills training and work experience and a number of social enterprises which employ young people.

Seamab Learning and Care Services (www.seamab.org.uk), which opened in 1988, is a fifteen-pupil residential primary school, located in a rural setting. Like Kibble, Seamab provides placements for extremely troubled children from across Scotland and also takes some day pupils who have a home base within travelling distance. Its care and education staff are supported by a team of psychologists, occupational and speech therapists and residential social workers who undertake therapeutic work with individual children. Its staff group have all been trained in 'dyadic developmental psychotherapy' (Hughes, 2009) to enable them to develop the kind of caring relationships that will meet each child's particular needs. Careful assessment of children means staff can develop individualised programmes of care, education and therapy.

CHAPTER 6

Daily Residential Practice in a Risk-Averse Environment

Introduction

In Chapter 5 we noted that all homes are required to have a statement of function and objectives intended to make residential staff teams more purposeful and focused, and to underpin the trend towards more specialist care with every unit focused on a specific area of practice. It was also expected that children would be placed in residential care according to their needs, ensuring that units are not merely 'holding' children. This aspiration, with its implication that every local authority would retain a range of different residential units, has been undermined as there has been a reduction in the overall number of residential places and homes and so differentiation of task is not much in evidence, apart from in close support units. The difficulty of identifying, and adhering to, specific remits has also been exacerbated by the high level of emergency placements that has become the norm, and the consequent pressure to use any available vacancy for children in crisis, leading to many local authority homes containing a mixture of children on short- and long-term placements (McPheat *et al.*, 2007). Despite the sometimes diverse requirements presented by any group of children, residential workers strive to provide for children's daily needs, creating an environment of personalised care and enabling children to live alongside one another with the aim of creating a familylike experience. Residential care is governed by the *National Care Standards* (Scottish Executive, 2005) and regularly inspected against them, and residential practice is informed by a number of theoretical approaches in meeting these standards. Scottish care standards are not 'minimum standards' – they are rather aspirational and wide ranging in their scope and language. Residential providers seek to provide the best possible care they can and often go beyond the terms of the care standards.

In this chapter we consider aspects of daily life within residential care and what it is that residential care workers try to achieve on a day-to-day basis. We also consider what theories or approaches to care may be influencing their practice and what external pressures or expectations may be shaping their environment.

Building on previous chapters, which have described the development of small-scale residential care units, this chapter explores how workers provide care in non-institutional forms while at the same time meeting social work agency demands and their own professional expectations about the aim or purpose of care placements. They also have meet the expectations of inspectors from the Care Inspectorate, who measure them against the *National Care Standards* (Scottish Executive, 2005).

The task of providing non-institutional care, or 'homely care' as it will be referred to, is made more complex by factors external to the child care system. These include the growing intrusion of actual or perceived 'health and safety' requirements and the associated practice of carrying out frequent risk assessments to manage the anxiety generated by an undue focus on hazards (Milligan, 2011). The emergence of risk-averse practice, often built on myths (HSE, 2010), has been noticed and lamented in several areas, particularly those providing services for children such as nurseries and schools (Gill, 2007; Piper *et al.*, 2006).

Homely and professional residential care

Family patterns are the reference point for contemporary residential care and not institutional or hospital ones. Even secure units – hybrid institutions containing elements of both prison and children's home – have high walls and locked internal doors, but also an internal environment with more homely norms. The physical environments of residential units are smaller, and children and young people normally have single bedrooms. As we have seen from descriptions of the creation of new children's houses, considerable thought has gone into making them comfortable and well-resourced, with high-quality decor and furnishings, and good facilities for study and recreation. At the same time, however, in most places the necessity of having an office and staff rooms emphasises that residential establishments are not just ordinary homes; they are also workplaces and often the sitting room or another public room will be used for meetings during the day.

Providing children with personal care in a warm, well-maintained environment, ensuring they have comfortable, clean clothes and access to plentiful, good-quality food are considered to be 'basic care' (Skinner, 1992). This kind of care is essential and should be taken for granted in a modern and well-resourced system. The way in which good basic care is given to youngsters who have experienced disruption and trauma should not be considered to be a 'basic' or simple task; it requires many skills, resilience and resourcefulness, including an ability to stand back and analyse situations, drawing on theories of child development and frameworks for practice, which may inform responses. Residential care also has many professional and therapeutic requirements that have to be integrated with the delivery of 'good basic care'. Creating an environment that is homely and nurturing, and that is also professional and purposeful, are the fundamental requirements of good residential child care.

Care has to be professional and purposeful because the children are not being cared for in the privacy of their own homes. They are subject to formal proceedings of courts and children's hearings and are allocated a social worker with statutory duties to carry out. Among these is devising a care plan (now known as the 'child's plan'), which must be reviewed at least every six months. The plan should be a 'live' document that informs the daily practice of all those involved with the child. Care plans are reviewed at formal meetings involving the child, family members, social workers, residential key-worker, a teacher and possibly also an independent 'advocate'.

Attending their 'review' is one of the most distinctive and difficult aspects of a child's life in care. Once they are old enough to understand what is going on, and to speak for themselves, children are expected to participate in these meetings, often held in the sitting room of the home where they are living in an attempt to make them more informal. In advance of the meeting reports are prepared by the social work and residential staff. These normally draw on assessment and planning tools from the *Getting It Right For Every Child* (GIRFEC) framework (Scottish Government, 2008a), and are designed to address all aspects of a child's life and their progress in relation to the issues identified in the care plan and to encourage planned inter-agency working. Children are invited to contribute their views about their own care experience and what they would like in their care plan.

Residential workers inhabit, and are responsible for, a world that aims to combine homely, nurturing, non-institutional care and purposeful, planned interventions. Combining these aspects is the challenge, and in the following section we identify some of the theoretical approaches that inform that task.

Lifespace

Ideas and practices associated with the term 'lifespace' offer a theoretical framework within which to approach the daily task of providing good basic care. It is a way of thinking about the conundrum of professional residential care: the residential home is both a place of work and a home, and the staff and children share this lifespace. Originating in the USA, and building on the work of Bruno Bettelheim and others, the idea has been a foundation for much theorising about residential child care. One current manifestation is a structured approach to behaviour management in residential settings, known as Therapeutic Crisis Intervention (TCI) (Holden, 2001).

The lifespace approach is a way of viewing the ordinary, routine events of daily life – sharing meals, bedtimes and recreation – and seeing the potential of these to be carried out in a way that is beneficial, or broadly therapeutic, to the young people. This includes providing daily experiences that give children a sense of security and predictability and above all being consistently looked after by adults who care about them. A lifespace approach to practice 'involves the conscious use of everyday events to promote the growth, development and learning of children and young people' (Smith, 2009, p. 1).

One of the insights of the lifespace approach is that daily life should be therapeutic. Using lifespace thinking helps workers reflect about the very ordinary interactions of life and to be aware that there may be different ways of getting children up in the morning, for example, or how to approach eating a meal together. Adrian Ward has developed a particular framework for understanding work in the lifespace that he calls 'opportunity-led practice' (Ward, 2007). He proposes that: 'even in the briefest of incidents' there are many interactions between children and carers and that these can be analysed in four stages: observation and assessment; decision-making; action; and closure (ibid., p. 64). Ward suggests that by, using this model, staff can be trained to develop their awareness and understanding and so respond to everyday events thoughtfully, rather than merely react to them since: 'it is in the handling of these unscheduled moments that many opportunities for useful communication (and some would say the 'real' work of group care) may arise' (ibid).

Building resilience

An important influence on residential child care is the developing interest in why some children appear to cope with serious adversity more successfully than others. A number of factors have been identified in more resilient children, and there has been a focus on trying to help build resilience in children in residential settings (Daniel and Wassell, 2002). Too often in children's homes there has been an overemphasis on the difficult lives of children and the consequent problems they experience without recognising and valuing the resources available to them and the skills they have developed, as demonstrated in the case study of David in Chapter 3. A strengths-based approach, which focuses on developing talents, reflective capacity, communication and problem-solving skills, can promote children's resilience (Gilligan, 2000). When carers and other children's services professionals work in this way, and children have secure relationships with adults and role models, the approach can have a cumulative, positive effect on their behaviour and social, cognitive and emotional abilities.

Resilience cannot develop without challenge, and the theoretical underpinning for this approach also emphasises the importance of children being exposed to manageable risk and stressors rather than being overprotected in a risk-averse environment. An interesting example of collaborative work to promote resilience among children in residential care involving teachers and residential workers has been developed from research by educational psychologists in South Lanarkshire Council. The approach, based on the work of Edith Grotberg ('I have, I am, I can'), uses a Framework of Assessment and Intervention for Resilience (FAIR) to help parents, carers, social workers and education staff to identify protective factors available to the child and to plan how best these can be mobilised in the interest of the child's development. (Psychologist Donna Carrigan explains the approach in a short podcast on the CELCIS website at www.celcis.org/resources/entry/donna_carrigan; accessed 5 July 2012.)

Safe care

It is important to acknowledge the changes that have occurred in relation to the organisation and management of residential child care over the past two decades. The issue of safeguarding children – preventing physical or sexual abuse – is a high-profile one given the publicity generated by reviews of abuse in residential settings within the UK, including the Edinburgh inquiry (Marshall *et al.*, 1999). The discovery of sustained abuse carried out by some carers, often remaining undetected for many years despite children's attempts to speak up, led to major reviews, such as the Kent report (Kent, 1997).

These reviews have led to the creation of a range of safeguarding measures intended to prevent abuse from occurring or at least allow its quicker detection, including:

- development of 'enhanced' police record checks for all staff prior to recruitment;
- more careful recruitment procedures generally including checking references;
- adoption of 'whistle-blowing' and complaints procedures;
- funding for independent advocacy services;
- development of National Care Standards and a national system of independent inspection (the Care Inspectorate), with its own complaints procedures;

- training and extensive guidance for staff on the use of physical restraint (Davidson *et al.*, 2005).

The most important 'safeguard' for children is the culture of a unit, which should be a positive and open one of care, provided by workers who feel empowered to question practice, supervised by managers who understand residential care and take ownership and responsibility for the development of the residential team and the quality of the care provided. Such a culture is marked by the willingness of residential staff to listen carefully to children, to challenge one another and to facilitate young people's access to independent advocacy.

Recreational activities

The provision of a range of recreational activities is an aspect of residential care practice that contributes to a positive care culture. Taking part in group games, learning how to kick or catch a ball, reaching the top of a hill, learning to swim, making a model or building a sandcastle can promote development across the physical, intellectual, emotional, social and spiritual domains. The organisation of outdoor recreation is an aspect of residential life that raises concerns about the perceived 'institutional' features of some activities, such as going on outings in groups. It is also a focus for anxiety about risks. Activities in this context usually include play and recreation outside the home whether individually, such as participating in a local sport or youth club, or as a group, going on a trip to a beach, to the cinema or to a football match. Activities may also include arts and crafts such as painting and model-making.

Activities as both homely and therapeutic

Encouraging a child to take up hobbies, or participate in sport, teaching a young child to play with others, or suggesting that a teenager might like to join a youth club or uniformed organisation are important ways of building social confidence. Such 'spare-time activities' are important in the development of resilience, providing opportunities and challenges that develop problem-solving, social skills and communication abilities (Gilligan, 2007). Promoting participation in social activities of one kind or another is very much a feature of contemporary family life and understood to be important for a child's healthy development.

When children's homes were larger it was inevitable that the children would most often play with each other, and there were many potential playmates close at hand. There was also a natural, if rather large, ready-made group for outings to the funfair or beach. Care has become more individual-oriented, and residential workers have been encouraged to avoid relying on organised group activities but to promote a child's own interests, especially where that involves engaging socially with friends.

Given the neglect and trauma that many looked after children have experienced, they are likely to lack social confidence, and to have little experience of the range of play and recreation opportunities available to their peers. Simply providing the opportunities will not be sufficient for many, and carers also have to be skilled in coaxing children with limited play experience and social skills to take part in new things.

Since many children placed in residential settings have experienced emotional difficulties associated with abuse, neglect and disruption to family life they are likely to have been left either socially isolated or introduced to a delinquent peer group. Workers engaging with such children see the therapeutic value of very ordinary, routine activities to help these children recover a positive sense of themselves and their capabilities, in what Bruno Bettelheim calls the 'in-between times' (Bettelheim, 1950). The provision of regular, well-supervised activities also has a role in preventing boredom and diverting young people from previous patterns of self-harming or anti-social behaviour. Even in today's small homes children are likely to make friends with each other, and a small group home does have many advantages in providing a ready-made social group, even if children do not become close friends. Outings from children's homes provide elements of a 'normal' home life, where trips and activities can be a source of tension as children have to learn to compromise and get along with others.

The North Lanarkshire children's houses described in Chapter 2 include a significant amount of internal and external space designed with play in mind, creating a home that has much to offer but is considerably larger than an average family home. The consultation process mentioned in that chapter elicited strong messages from children about a lack of things to do. In their bold designs, which included a large open-plan living space in the centre of the home, the architects created distinct spaces for computers, a TV lounging area, a quiet zone and a dining area. The garden was carefully planned to have distinct recreational zones, including a grass, kick-about area, hard standing with a basketball hoop and decking for a barbecue, with softer landscaping provided by flower beds and shrubbery. Is this environment homely or institutional? Is it possible to be both?

Risk-aversion and activities

There is, however, another side to the challenge of providing normal recreational activities in a group care context, and that is the concern about minimising risk and the expectation that everything should be risk-assessed. This practice has grown up in many fields, especially those involving children: for example, schools are often expected to undertake written risk assessments for activities or situations that were previously seen as the responsibility of an individual teacher, or head teacher, requiring no formal written checks, merely the application of common sense. The related issue of getting permission to undertake outdoor activities appears to have hindered residential staff from acting naturally and spontaneously (Milligan and Stevens, 2006).

Many residential workers and social workers believed (erroneously) that the permission of the residential carer was not sufficient to allow a child to go on a school trip, for example, and that consent forms had to be signed by birth parents. The routine use of formal 'risk assessment' procedures for everyday activities such as riding a bicycle is a barrier to normal childhood, and the *National Care Standards* state that children should be kept safe 'but not be overprotected' (Scottish Executive, 2005, pp. 7–8).

It is a challenge for managers to practise proportionate risk management while at the same time encouraging spontaneous and natural forms of recreation with children who may be resistant to taking part in them. Risk-aversion in residential settings is understandable, as this quotation taken from *Go Outdoors!* shows:

> Risk-averse practice is not just about fear of the worse possible scenario. It is also about the fact that everyone tends to be more cautious when looking after other people's

children. In residential care, this feeling is even more heightened. The young residents are 'other people's children' (SIRCC, 2010a).

The 'worst possible scenario' referred to is the death or serious injury of a child while in care in circumstances that a later inquiry might judge were the result of negligence on the part of workers. It is right and proper that children should not be taken into the hills, for example, by workers who do not have the correct qualifications and experience.

This caution is, however, overlain by two particular problems. One is the tendency for sensible guidance intended for one condition to become generalised to all situations. It is not necessary to have a mountain leader qualification to take children low-level walking in well-signposted woodland, although even that less hazardous activity requires careful planning and consideration of possible risks. The second problem is the extent to which myths are perpetuated about what can or cannot be done. An example is the apparently common belief that children in care could not paddle while at a beach unless workers present had lifeguard qualifications. The problem for workers is that sometimes myths are perpetuated by managers or others with more power to circumscribe activities.

A worker at a children's unit was an enthusiastic gardener and encouraged children to grow vegetables. A council environmental officer, on a routine visit to the home, informed the staff that the vegetables could not be eaten because they were not from a traceable source. This was erroneous advice, but the workers felt powerless because of the official's status. The ruling was later successfully challenged; the official had misunderstood his department's guidance which had in fact been written for homes for the elderly and was intended as a sensible precaution for the supply of cooked and uncooked meats. The important message for residential workers and managers is to become familiar with their organisation's guidance and not to rely on second-hand interpretations, which might be inaccurate.

The common third

Within the philosophy and practice of social pedagogy (a term referring to an approach to group care that straddles social work and
education) a particular way of conceptualising recreation has been
developed, known as the 'common third'. This way of thinking proposes that activities can be considered to be positive and relational if
they are truly shared and enjoyed by both the carer and the child; the
activity becomes the 'third' thing with the adult and child:

> Essentially the Common Third is about using an activity to
> strengthen the bond between social pedagogue and child
> and to develop new skills. This could be any activity, be it
> cooking pancakes, tying shoelaces, fixing a bike, building
> a kite, playing football together, or going on a fishing trip
> together. Any of these activities can be so much more than
> doing something – it is about creating a commonly shared
> situation that becomes a symbol of the relationship between
> the social pedagogue and the child, something 'third' that
> brings the two together ... to have something in common,
> implies in principle to be equal, to be two (or more) indi-
> viduals on equal terms, with equal rights and dignity (Eich-
> steller, 2009, p. 1).

These insights provide a theoretical framework for thinking about,
and encouraging, the kinds of activities that residential workers have
often done. The introduction of social pedagogy, an approach with
its origins in continental Europe, into the UK has resulted in at least
some residential workers taking children outdoors with a new confidence. At heart the social pedagogy approach encourages residential
workers, and all professionals engaged in direct work with children, to
see themselves as responsible for the healthy development of the child,
and it affirms the role that their personal relationship and shared
interest can play. Concerns about 'health and safety' are not abandoned but rather put into a more appropriate context.

Two leading writers about social pedagogy have proposed that the
task of residential workers is to promote 'risk competence' among the
children they are responsible for, rather than pursing the illusory goal

of keeping children safe by writing up risk assessments for everyday activities, with the implication that all risks can be avoided (Eichsteller and Holthoff, 2009).

Promoting the education of children in care

The 2001 *Learning with Care* report resulted from an inspection of the education of fifty children in residential care settings in five of Scotland's thirty-two local authorities. It is highly critical of the lack of attention given to the education of children in care, including inadequate conditions for doing homework, lack of detailed attention to educational needs in care plans and poor liaison with schools (HMI/SWSI, 2001; Maclean and Gunion, 2003). The report advocates that a residential children's home should aspire to be an 'educationally rich environment', a useful concept in countering unstimulating intellectual conditions and low educational expectations of looked after children.

In the years since 2001 considerable attention has been given to the education of looked after children, in legislative, policy and practice terms, as outlined in Chapter 4. But what can residential workers do themselves to promote learning, school attendance and high aspiration? Care leavers who have done well in education often point to the encouragement and practical help they received from an individual worker or teacher (Happer *et al.*, 2006). It is important to have appropriate expectations for children and also to plan actively for their achievement.

Workers can show they value learning in the widest sense by talking openly about their own studies if they are doing a course, by offering to tutor if they have particular subject expertise and by organising visits to museums, art galleries and cultural events during leisure time. They can develop good relationships with the schools or colleges attended by the children and young people, and work proactively to avoid exclusions and ensure that additional support needs are addressed without delay. Some workers find this aspect of the work challenging, particularly if their own experience of education was not positive, and they need support from managers to develop the necessary skills; nevertheless it is essential they realise that attending to the education of children is a vital part of their caring role.

It is possible for workers deliberately to develop a culture that values education in a children's home (Gallagher *et al.*, 2004). Research funded by the Scottish government reviewed pilot projects in eighteen local authorities aimed at improving the educational attainment of looked after children; one of the findings was that staff who believed in the children they were working with treated them with respect, had high expectations for them and were more able to engage children successfully in their education (Connelly *et al.*, 2008). The government published advice for local authorities, based on the research, about planning for improving the educational experience of looked after children (Connelly and Furnivall, 2009).

One very high profile way of demonstrating high academic aspirations for children in care is the annual scholarship provided by Who Cares? Scotland to support a young person to attend the Harvard University summer school (Cosh, 2010).

Promoting health

This is a broad topic that includes ensuring children in care have health assessments that are carried out sensitively, supporting children who may have aversions to receiving treatment and encouraging healthy lifestyles in the home setting. Specialist, looked after children's nurses perform an important role in identifying previously unmet needs, compiling individual health plans and providing direct healthcare, such as smoking cessation assistance and sexual health advice. They can also be invaluable allies in liaising with medical colleagues, many of whom will not have direct knowledge or understanding of looked after children, and may even have unhelpful attitudes, such as the optician who refused to make a domiciliary visit to a secure unit because 'we do not attend inmates in penal institutes' (Wilson, 2009, p. 35).

Workers themselves have an important role in promoting health, not only by performing direct care tasks, such as ensuring children brush their teeth and get help with health problems such acne, but also in modelling healthy lifestyles. For example, it is regarded as best practice for a worker who smokes not to do so in view of children. Also, a worker who is intent on giving up could consider joining a cessation programme along with young smokers. Workers can participate in exercise or sport with young people. Staff teams should consider the importance of food practices, healthy eating and meal routines in residential life (Punch *et al.*, 2009). Workers have a special role in supporting children with a history of abuse who may have particular fears about visits to the doctor or dentist. This skilled work could include liaising with the medical or dental practitioner to discuss the child's concerns and to offer advice on sensitive approaches.

Working with the impact of trauma

Most young people who spend significant amounts of time in residential care will have been exposed to trauma, often in their earliest childhood. Recent developments in neuroscience have made it clear that emotional trauma has a direct impact on brain functioning, and if it occurs in the time between conception and age three is likely to have serious effects on the development of the brain's architecture (Perry, 2009).

The implications of early developmental trauma on children's capacity to regulate their behaviour are profound, and such children are likely to struggle with the everyday demands of childhood – school, friendships, participation in sports or other activities. Children's homes can be organised in a 'trauma sensitive' way, which ensures that the physical and sensory environment is soothing rather than likely to create triggers for highly aroused children. Residential workers are becoming more aware of their responsibility to provide respectful but compensatory experiences that address the developmental rather than chronological age of the children in their care and ensure that they are able to recover from the trauma they may have experienced earlier in their lives.

Records and reports

One factor that makes life in residential or foster care strikingly different for children – no matter how homely the physical environment – is that their lives are recorded in detail. It is established practice in residential care that a daily note, or log, is written up about each child by workers on every shift. These notes are likely to cover routine things such as a record of a child's illnesses and also their behaviour, especially if a problem has arisen at school or in the home.

There are various purposes for this kind of intensive record keeping in residential care. One of the most important is simply to inform good and consistent care. In a shift system, information needs to be written down so that incoming staff know what has happened while they have not been there. The ready availability of detailed records of significant events and incidents also creates a good basis for retrospectively reflecting on children's behaviour and needs and considering how best to work together to support their development. Another reason for keeping detailed daily records is to monitor the care plan, which forms a key part of the care context. The daily record affords a means to monitor the child's progress and acts as a source of information about important decisions, such as whether they should remain in care or are ready to move or back to parents.

Having daily living experiences recorded is a feature of life in care that is very different from life in a family home, but it is intended that recording should promote the best possible individual or personal care. Record keeping should be done in a transparent way, and children have a right to see what is written about them. In some homes these daily records will be shared with the children – if they are interested – as they are being written, and in recent years workers have been encouraged to record positive experiences rather than merely to note the troubles and negative incidents, which can too easily become the focus of attention. It is important to think carefully about the purpose of record keeping – that is the communication of information vital for good care – and to consider that having a lot of unimportant details in files may make it difficult for professionals to locate vital information.

Summary

This purpose of this chapter was to introduce the reader to the complex nature of residential care practice by discussing some of its everyday tasks. The chapter drew attention to what makes residential work attractive and rewarding, and demonstrated how it can be challenging to provide daily care and activities that are both normal and therapeutic. We have also shown that providing good care can be frustrated by undue concern about risk.

Thinking outside the box: Therapeutic care, sanctions and football

If you are working with children and young people in any setting school, youth club, foster-family or group care, you have to manage behaviour. Think about your experience of discipline and boundary setting. Do you think children can or should be disciplined the way you were? The use of 'punishments' or 'sanctions' in nursery, school or care settings has generally been discouraged, while instead 'consequences' is regarded as more acceptable. How would you describe the difference between these terms? Might there be negative impacts of withholding resilience-building activities as a consequence for difficult behaviours?

In the extract below Laura Steckley reflects on the importance of activities, especially football, in a boys' residential school where she worked, and the complexity of applying sanctions or consequences when they misbehaved:

> At my school not a day went by without one or more requests to go the games hall or pitch for a kick-about. For a majority of the boys, football was a daily focus, both in terms of its general desirability for fun and energy release, and as an ongoing investment in developing skills for performance on the team …
>
> Activities have no rival in terms of a sense of mastery and self-esteem, and can prevent the all too often adversarial climate that can develop between staff and young people … In terms of how notions of resiliency relate to the football team, it is clear that for most of the boys who participate in the school team, this is an opportunity in the week (maybe the only one) where they feel like they are good at something, that something is of significant value in their world, and they are part of something successful …
>
> An adult [may] fall back on the worn-out 'that'll be you not playing football this week if you don't get back to class', in an attempt to manage a young people's acting out behaviour …
>
> A residential setting must hold its young people accountable for their actions if it is to provide a safe environment and promote the development of self-control. How this is done effectively, especially with young people who have not previously experienced boundaries and accountability in a safe and consistent (if at all), is extremely complex (Steckley, 2005).

CHAPTER 7

Group Care for Children and the Emergence of Social Pedagogy

Introduction

In this chapter we consider the relative neglect of the group aspect of residential care, both in theory and practice – a consequence surely of the focus on avoiding institutional practices and focusing on individual care plans. Social pedagogy is beginning to make an impact in Scotland, perhaps because it affirms the group aspect of care and offers a theoretical framework for reflecting on the role of a professional child and youth care worker in the residential context. We will suggest that social pedagogy can build on the best-quality residential care in Scotland and provide a sound framework for training residential workers. In doing so we hope that we are, at least in part, meeting the challenge to engage in the wider 'moral and political debate' envisaged by Mark Smith:

> [T]he ecology within which residential child care currently exists is not always conducive to effective or ethical practice. Maximising what residential child care might offer to children requires a more fundamental rethink. This in turn requires those who assert a positive role for residential child care to engage in moral and political debate about the possibilities of the sector rather than becoming caught up in the search for ever more prescriptive technical and administrative fixes (Smith, 2009, p. 1).

By now the reader will be aware that we count ourselves among those who 'assert a positive role' for the sector. The NRCCI chose optimistic language for the title of its series of reports, *Higher Aspirations, Brighter Futures*. As noted in Chapter 4, these reports called for radical changes, including a wider role for residential care (encompassing earlier intervention to prevent long-term care, and higher-level training for staff) among other recommendations. The *Overview* report asserted that 'we need to change the culture in which it is delivered' (Bayes, 2009, p. 14), echoing Smith's (2009) emphasis on the need for changes in the 'ecology' or system in which residential care operates and not just on the internal organisation or staffing of residential units.

The current form of residential child care is perhaps less visible and less well known to the wider public than were the former, large children's homes and 'approved' schools. Certainly, the professional function and approach of the homes are little known or understood, and residential workers are often dealing with suspicion from neighbours, public ignorance and sometimes professional scepticism about their role. There have been campaigns against the opening of new homes as local residents have expressed fears about the effects on their neighbourhoods, as illustrated in this newspaper headline: 'Fury at plan to re-open the Hell Home' (Clackson *et al.*, 2006, p. 33).

Despite more open discussion about child neglect and abuse, the perceptions that children in care must be 'bad' and that they are likely to cause more trouble than other children are pervasive. The plaintive cry in the quotation below is indicative of the stigma that some young people and their families experience:

> Spread the word that it's not children's fault for being in children's homes because they think it's you and you've done something wrong, but for us it was our parents that had the problem and not us. The minute people look at you, they look with disgust, and they say that you're in a bad boys' or a bad girls' home, as if to say you have done something really violent, and we haven't done anything wrong' (Paterson *et al.*, 2003, p. 13).

Simplistic views that portray children from troubled homes and disadvantaged communities as either victims (especially younger children) or delinquents (especially older children) persist.

In writing this book we hope to counter some of that lack of understanding, at least among children's services professionals and students. We want to promote understanding of this relatively small yet vitally important part of the world of child care and social services. A central part of that task has been to show how group care has been driven by the desire for it to be 'homely' in size, design and decor, calibrated by familial scale rather than institutional features. The corresponding approach to residential care practice has been to eschew all forms of routine or group work in favour of individualising care through an individual child's plan and the key-worker role. Residential care is clearly not a standard type of family life and yet neither is foster care; perhaps too much stress has been placed on the differences between them. Young people have often voiced their preference for residential care over foster care (Milligan and Stevens, 2006) and instability in foster care is increasingly a matter of concern.

Neglect of the 'group' in residential care

While we have no disagreement with the humanistic intent and aspiration behind the trend for small-scale care and individual care planning, nevertheless, the reluctance to find a positive philosophy of group care and models of practice is notable. Most of the direction at a practice level has been to avoid institutional responses in favour of individual ones, and only recently have some units, mainly in the voluntary and private sectors, begun to adopt group care methods and theoretical frameworks for practice (Milligan and Furnivall, 2011). This is despite the statutory requirement for homes to have a statement of functions and objectives (see Chapter 5), which includes a philosophy of care. With a few exceptions, there has been a lack of theoretical framing in which good practice can be measured, other than the avoidance of institutional care as a guiding principle.

Work at the level of 'group', an essential aspect of residential care, has been managed largely on the basis of practice wisdom and experience, and has not had a sufficient theoretical foundation that would allow residential workers to maintain a focus on children's needs and development when faced with anxieties about child protection or managing risks. There has been little guidance telling people what to do in terms of positive group care practice, rather than what not to do. The exception is the small number of writers who since the early 1980s have been conceptualising residential child care as a form of 'group care'.

Leon Fulcher and Frank Ainsworth edited two volumes that built on the ideas of Henry Maier and others about the therapeutic use of daily living – the lifespace approach – referred to in Chapter 6 (Ainsworth and Fulcher, 1981; Fulcher and Ainsworth, 2006). Ruth Emond carried out an ethnographic study of children's experience of group care by living full-time in two children's homes for six months (Emond, 2004). She identified the ways in which young people supported each other through the experience of being in a home and proposed the idea of 'currencies' to describe the particular strengths valued by children and young people in the group care context. In *Working in Group Care* Adrian Ward sought to provide analytical frameworks for practice, recognising common elements between the care of groups of service users of all ages, whether in residential or day care group settings (Ward, 2007). In explaining the nature of group care and its significance Ward argues that it is defined by skilled use of daily living situations:

> What is promoted by the use of the concept of group care, then, is the recognition that this creative exploiting of the opportunities for change and growth that arise in daily living is a valid method of social work, which happens in both residential and day care work but not normally (or not so fully) in other methods of social work (Ward, 2007, p. 7).

Training of residential staff and the emergence of social pedagogy in the UK

Group care was a major curriculum topic in the Certificate in Social Service (CSS), a professional qualification for residential and day care staff that was available from 1975 to 1995. It had been developed by the government-funded social work training body, the Central Council for Education and Training in Social Work (CCETSW). The CSS and the main qualification for social workers, the Certificate of Qualification in Social Work (CQSW), were both replaced by the higher-level Diploma in Social Work (DipSW). Following the loss of the CSS it became difficult to retain residential workers who gained the DipSW, as many moved into fieldwork, an environment where everybody was qualified, salaries were higher and normal working hours applied. There was also a continuing questioning of the extent to which the typical DipSW course adequately valued and prepared students for residential work (Lane, 1994; NISW, 1998).

The fact that the philosophy and profession of social pedagogy existed in mainland Europe and was the normal form of training for residential workers continued to be explored, or at least mentioned, whenever the training of residential workers in the UK was discussed: for example, by Warner in his report into recruitment and selection of staff (Warner, 1992). The Skinner report in Scotland (Skinner, 1992) and the Utting report in England and Wales (Utting, 1991) led to funding for the training of residential child care workers using adapted DipSW courses (Lane, 1994). Roger Kent, in his wide-ranging review of 'safeguarding' in residential child care in Scotland, considered whether social pedagogy might be the way ahead for the education of residential workers but instead promoted the 'specialist pathway' option under the DipSW, which has been provided in Scotland (Kent, 1997). Nevertheless, the number of residential staff gaining a social work qualification has not increased significantly since 2000 (Lerpiniere et al., 2007).

Into this gap has come a growing interest in social pedagogy and the recent emergence of social pedagogy degree programmes (e.g. at Robert Gordon and Aberdeen universities), which have been accredited by the SSSC as recognised professional qualifications for social care workers.

What is social pedagogy?

There is a growing literature on the conceptual underpinnings and practice development of social pedagogy, an example of which is the edited collection by Claire Cameron and Peter Moss, *Social Pedagogy and Working with Children and Young People: Where Care and Education Meet* (Cameron and Moss, 2011). It is important to recognise that there is no single social pedagogy, as the approach has evolved somewhat differently in each of the countries in which it is found.

Social pedagogy essentially describes the way societies think about children, their education and their upbringing. One definition is 'education in the widest sense ... a holistic approach to a child's upbringing' (Cameron and Moss, 2011, pp. 8–9). Social pedagogy therefore is not, like social work, mainly about the implementation of statutory duties. It has been adopted eagerly in the UK, particularly by those groups of workers who do 'direct work' with children and young people – residential workers and early years workers – as it offers a way of thinking about the 'lifespace' where children live or spend considerable periods of time.

Although different in their main focus – since social pedagogues tend not to be based in offices or to carry out statutory casework – social work and social pedagogy nevertheless have a lot in common. Both are rooted in personal welfare, and practitioners are involved in the lives of vulnerable, excluded or disabled groups. There is a considerable interaction between social work and social pedagogy in those countries where both are established, and there is also a growing literature in English that seeks to explore what social pedagogy may have to offer to social work in the UK (Hamalainen, 2003).

Research undertaken at the Thomas Coram Research Unit (TCRU) at the University of London has identified the following key principles of social pedagogy practice:

- a focus on the child as a whole person, and support for the child's overall development;
- the practitioner seeing herself/himself as a person, in relationship with the child or young person;
- while they are together, children and staff are seen as inhabiting the same lifespace, not as existing in separate, hierarchical domains;
- as professionals, pedagogues are encouraged to constantly reflect on their practice and to apply both theoretical understandings and self-knowledge to their work and to the sometimes challenging demands with which they are confronted;
- pedagogues should be both practical and creative; their training prepares them to share in many aspects of children's daily lives, such as preparing meals and snacks, or making music and building kites;

- in group settings, children's associative life is seen as an important resource: workers should foster and make use of the group;
- pedagogy builds on an understanding of children's rights that is not limited to procedural matters or legislative requirements;
- there is an emphasis on team work and valuing the contributions of others – family members, other professionals and members of the local community – in the task of 'bringing up' children (Petrie *et al.*, 2009, p. 3).

The relevance of these features to child care is obvious, especially the affirmation of the group.

A number of local authorities and other providers of residential care have begun to train staff through in-service programmes. In England the government funded a major pilot programme using social pedagogues largely recruited from Germany and Denmark to work in children's homes for a two-year period in order to provide fresh thinking about residential care and model social pedagogy approaches (Cameron *et al.*, 2011).

A useful collection of information about social pedagogy among practitioners working in a range of contexts is Social Pedagogy UK, a commercially sponsored website that includes a forum for discussion (see www.socialpedagogyuk.com).

What is the impact of social pedagogy?
As social pedagogy is still relatively uncommon in the UK, the development of training for residential workers has been largely influenced by experience from elsewhere in Europe, such as Germany and Denmark. In these countries, degree-level education is more accessible than in the UK, where the dissemination of social pedagogic theory and practice has depended largely on short-course training provided by local authorities and third-sector organisations. There is evidence that the approach appeals to practitioners and among the positive features of social pedagogy identified by participants are:

- residential workers find that being introduced to social pedagogy concepts and approaches builds their confidence in the job;

- they are encouraged to reflect more on themselves and on understanding children's behaviour, 'standing back' rather than 'jumping in' too quickly when difficult situations arise;
- they are doing more with young people in terms of activities, especially outdoor activities;
- social pedagogy can provide a very helpful framework and shared language for thinking about the needs of vulnerable or challenging children (Milligan, 2009; Vrouwenfelder *et al.*, 2012).

Workers report that social pedagogy appeals to them because it provides a framework for bringing together the different aspects of their role. In particular, it affirms the personal dimension of the work, and encourages them to take more responsibility for the child or young person's overall development.

There has been a tendency to use a simplistic contrast between the professional and the personal in UK social work. Social pedagogy by contrast introduces workers to three dimensions: private, personal and professional. Using this framework it is argued that, while there is a private realm of experience that is not usually brought into the workplace, the personal is central to the relational work that the worker is expected to do. The professional dimension is also present, but social pedagogues understand the way that the personal and the professional dimensions are deployed in relationships with children and colleagues.

Social pedagogy has also reintroduced the idea of working with children using 'head, hands and heart', the last dimension emphasising the emotional engagement with another person that is vital to authentic care relationships (Boddy, 2011).

> Social Pedagogy, it could be argued, is all about 'being' – about being with others and forming relationships, being in the present and focusing on initiating learning processes, being authentic and genuine, using one's own personality, and about being there in a supportive, empowering manner. As such, social pedagogy is like an art form: it's not just a skill to learn but needs to be brought to life through the

social pedagogue's *Haltung* – her attitude or mind set (Bird and Eichsteller, 2011, p. 1).

In other words, social pedagogy is not so much about what you do, but 'how' you do it. This perspective of social pedagogy means that it is dynamic, creative and process-orientated rather than mechanical, procedural and automated. This means a social pedagogue is required to be a whole person and not just a pair of hands.

Summary

In this chapter we have made the point that, despite residential care being representative of all care for looked after children in public perception (the 'Tracy Beaker' view of care), in fact the work done in modern residential homes remains largely hidden to a wider public. We have also suggested that the explicit move away from institutionalisation towards more individualised forms of residential care may have suffered from a lack of attention to the philosophy or theory of care to guide its practice. In response to this omission, we introduced the approach of social pedagogy, which offers a more holistic approach to the child's upbringing. We argued that social pedagogy has the dual advantage of affirming the professionalism of the residential worker and also of emphasising the importance of workers taking responsibility for the child's overall development.

Some might be unconcerned that residential child care is a small part of the child care sector, and indeed that it is reducing as a proportion of the whole. It could be claimed that residential care has become more appropriately targeted and that children who do not need residential placements are not referred to them. But, as we have argued elsewhere in this book, residential care is often used as a fall-back option when other placements do not work and significant numbers of children are placed on an unplanned basis and often for short periods of a few days or weeks.

This book has given an overview of residential child care in Scotland today, now universally provided in domestic-scale environments for small groups of children and young people. While there should be critical appraisal of residential practice and an acceptance of the need to make improvements, it is clear to us that the most important change required is the way residential care is perceived by professionals and the wider public. Such change should involve an appreciation of the positive role of the (small) group aspect of care, and helping residential workers to develop understandings of the use of authentic relationships with children and young people living in this context. The incorporation of concepts and practices drawn from social pedagogy is showing considerable promise in equipping workers and agencies to improve residential practice and to advocate for more effective use of residential care.

There is a great danger that society sleepwalks into a situation in which the residential sector declines to an extent that it is not viable and the possibility of making a positive choice of group care for a child is not available. In writing this book we have argued against simplistic notions that unconditionally favour family settings over group settings. There will always be a need for a range of care options available to children's panels when considering the best possible placement for an individual child. We think that the deliberate practice of avoiding placing younger children in residential settings and preferring foster placements has been unnecessarily limiting and has contributed to the view that residential placements should be used when family settings are not available or have broken down.

Residential homes and schools offer a warm and skilled 'embrace' to children and young people in the midst of crisis, emotional chaos and physical danger. High-quality residential care offers many advantages for looked after children. First, its very existence provides choice of care setting and recognises that some young people prefer group care to family-type settings. Secondly, it is a misunderstanding to assume that group care is more anonymous and does not allow children to develop close attachments to carers. There are advantages in the group setting where children have physical and emotional space to develop healing relationships without feeling trapped in a family that is attempting to replace their own. Thirdly, the emergence of a view of residential settings within a broad continuum of services, as envisaged by the NRCCI, offers opportunities for better co-operation between residential and foster care (Hill, 2009). Finally, the existence of a vibrant residential care sector is the best guarantee of having a properly professional workforce.

Workers do not replace birth parents, and the job is not simply parenting, since responding to the needs of children who have experienced neglect and trauma requires thorough preparation, deep understanding of child development and a sophisticated set of practice skills. The NRCCI recommended degree-level education as the minimum preparation for residential work. Although possession of formal qualifications is not the only quality needed in a good carer, such a requirement is at least a recognition that the work is as complex as, say, teaching or nursing.

We said at the beginning of this book that our aim was to leave the reader better informed about residential care for looked after children and feeling better placed to ask questions about its contribution to services for children. We hope we have given children's views and experiences a central place in our descriptions and analyses, and been open about our own values and assumptions. Scotland has much to be proud of in the way that its residential child care services have adapted to the challenges of recent years. A 'market' has developed and the number of small-scale providers has increased, but overall the sector has continued to contract while the need for more care options for children has increased. There are many examples of innovation in practice but little evidence of strategic development that recognises the importance of residential care within a spectrum of provision. Much work remains to be done to provide stability in the system and a consistent quality of care in the service of children and their families.

REFERENCES

Ainsworth, F. and Fulcher, L. (eds) (1981) *Group Care for Children: Concept and Issues*, London: Tavistock Publications

Ainsworth, F. and Hansen, P. (2011) 'Residential programs for children and young people: Their current status and use in Australia', in Courtney, M. and Iwaniec, D. (eds) (2011) *Residential Care of Children: Comparative Perspectives*, New York: Oxford University Press, pp. 139–53

Asquith, S. (1995) *The Kilbrandon Report: Children and Young Persons Scotland*. Edinburgh: HMSO. Available at URL: www.scotland.gov.uk/Resource/Doc/47049/0023863.pdf (accessed 26 June 2012)

Audit Scotland (2010) *Getting It Right for Children in Residential Care*. Edinburgh: Audit Scotland. Available at URL: www.audit-scotland.gov.uk/docs/local/2010/nr_100902_children_residential.pdf (accessed 17 July 2012)

Barnardo's Scotland (2012) 'Barnardo's Scotland response to the Scottish Government mental health consultation'. Available at URL: www.barnardos.org.uk/barnardo_s_scotland_response_to_the_scottish_government_s_mental_health_consultation-_jan2012.pdf (accessed 26 June 2012)

Bayes, K. (2009) *Higher Aspirations, Brighter Futures: National Residential Child Care Initiative Overview Report*, Glasgow: SIRCC. Available at URL: www.celcis.org/media/resources/publications/F1.pdf (accessed 17 July 2012)

Berridge, D., Dance, C., Beecham, J. and Field, S. (2008) *Educating Difficult Adolescents: Effective Education for Children in Public Care or With Emotional and Behavioural Difficulties*, London: Jessica Kingsley

Bettelheim, B. (1950) *Love Is Not Enough*, Glencoe, IL: Free Press

Bird, V. and Eichsteller, G. (2011) 'The relevance of social pedagogy in working with young people in residential care', *Good Enough Caring Journal*, Vol. 9, No. 10. Available at URL: www.goodenoughcaring.com/JournalArticle.aspx?cpid=155 (accessed 26 June 2012)

Boddy, J. (2011) 'The supportive relationship in public care: The relevance of social pedagogy', in Cameron, C. and Moss, P. (eds), *Social Pedagogy and Working With Children and Young People*, London: Jessica Kingsley, pp. 105–24

Bolger, J. and Miller, J. (2012) 'Residential child care in practice', in Davis, M. (ed.), *Social Work With Children and Families,* Basingstoke: Palgrave, pp. 304–22

Browne, K., Hamilton-Giachritsis, C., Johnson, R. and Ostergren, M. (2006) 'Overuse of institutional care for children in Europe', *BMJ, Vol.* 332, No. 7539, pp. 485–7; doi: 10.1136/bmj.332.7539.485

Cameron, C. and Moss, P. (eds). (2011) *Social Pedagogy and Working With Children and Young People: Where Care and Education Meet*, London: Jessica Kingsley

Cameron, C., Petrie, P., Wigfall, V., Kleipoedszus, S. and Jasper, A. (2011) *Final Report of the Social Pedagogy Pilot Programme: Development and Implementation*, London: TCRU. Available at URL: http://eprints.ioe.ac.uk/6767/1/Cameron2011Final(Report).pdf (accessed 17 July 2012)

Care Commission (2004) *A Review of the Quality of Care Homes in Scotland 2004*, Dundee: Scottish Commission for the Regulation of Care. Available at URL: www.scswis.com/index2.php?option=com_docman&task=doc_view&gid=272&Itemid=703 (accessed 17 July 2012)

Care Commission (2010) *Care Commission Quality Review 2002–10: Supplementary Tables*. Dundee: Care Commission. Available at URL: www.scswis.com/index.php?option=com_docman&task=doc_details&gid=258&Itemid=703 (accessed 17 July 2012)

Care Commission and Her Majesty's Inspectors of Schools (2005) *Residential Care and Education: Improving Practice in Residential Special Schools in Scotland*. Edinburgh: HMIE. Available at URL: www.scswis.com/index2.php?option=com_docman&task=doc_view&gid=271&Itemid=378 (accessed 17 July 2012)

Carter, R. (2005) *Family Matters: A Study of Institutional Childcare in Central and Eastern Europe and the Former Soviet Union*, London: Every Child. Available at URL: http://p-ced.com/reference/Family_Matters_summary.pdf (accessed 17 July 2012)

Clackson, A., Lindsay, S. and Macquarrie, A. (2006) 'The homes from hell? Media perceptions of residential child care', *Scottish Journal of Residential Child Care*, Vol. 5, No. 1, pp. 25–36. Available at URL: www.celcis.org/resources/entry/scottish_journal_of_residential_child_care_vol_5.1_feb_mar_2006 (accessed 18 July 2012)

Clements, D. (2007) 'The state of parenting'. Available at URL: http://daveclements.net (accessed 26 June 2012)

Connelly, G., Forrest, J., Furnivall, J., Siebelt, L., Smith, I. and Seagraves, L. (2008) *The Educational Attainment of Looked After Children Local Authority Pilot Projects: Final Research Report*. Edinburgh: Scottish Government. Available at URL: www.scotland.gov.uk/Publications/2008/09/12095701/0 (accessed 26 June 2012)

Connelly, G. and Furnivall, J. (2009) *Improving the Education of Looked After Children: A Guide For Local Authorities and Service Providers*. Edinburgh: Scottish Government. Available at URL: www.scotland.gov.uk/Publications/2009/03/25142835/0 (accessed 26 June 2012)

Cosh, J. (2010) 'On course for the heights of Harvard', *Times Educational Supplement Scotland,* 4 September. Available at URL: www.tes.co.uk/article.aspx?storycode=6058949 (accessed 17 July 2012)

Crimmens, D. and Milligan, I. (2005) 'Residential child care: Becoming a positive choice', in Crimmens, D. and Milligan, I. (eds) (2005) *Facing Forward: Residential Child Care in the 21st Century*, Lyme Regis: Russell House

Cross, C. (2011) 'Residential child care in the 1960s and now: Some comparisons', *Good Enough Caring Journal*, Vol. 11. Available at URL: www.goodenoughcaring.com (accessed 17 July 2012)

Daniel, B. and Wassell, S. (2002) *Assessing and Promoting Resilience in Vulner-*

able Children: Adolescence, London: Jessica Kingsley

Davidson, J. (2010) 'Residential care for children and young people: Priority areas for change', *Child Abuse Review*, Vol. 19, No. 6, pp. 405–22; doi: 10.1002/car.1137

Davidson, J., McCullough, D., Steckley, L. and Warren, T. (2005) *Holding Safely: A Guide for Residential Child Care Practitioners and Managers About Physically Restraining Children and Young People*. Glasgow: Scottish Institute for Residential Child Care, Scottish Executive, Social Work Inspection Agency. Available at URL: www.celcis.org/resources/holding_safely_2005 (accessed 18 July 2012)

Davidson, J., Wilkinson, C., Docherty, B. and Anderson, M. (2009) *Higher Aspirations, Brighter Futures: NRCCI Workforce Report*, Glasgow: Scottish Institute for Residential Child Care. Available at URL: www.celcis.org/media/resources/publications/F4.pdf (accessed 17 July 2012)

Docherty, C., Kendrick, A., Sloan, P. and Lerpiniere, J. (2006) *Designing with Care: Interior Design and Residential Care*, Glasgow: Farm 7/Scottish Institute for Residential Child Care. Available at URL: www.scotland.gov.uk/Publications/2006/06/SprDwc (accessed 17 July 2012)

DOH (1998) *Caring For Children Away From Home: Messages From Research,* London: Department of Health

DOH (2004) *The Quality Protects Programme: Transforming Children's Services*. London: Department of Health. Available at URL: www.dh.gov.uk/en/Publicationsandstatistics/Lettersandcirculars/Healthservicecirculars/DH_4003877 (accessed 26 June 2012)

Downey, L., Gibson, B. and Dini, P. K. (2011) 'The Cape Kids' service', *Relational Child and Youth Care Practice*, Vol. 24, Nos 1–2, pp. 142–7.

Duncalf, Z. (2010) 'Listen up! adult care leavers speak out: The views of 310 care leavers aged 17–78'. Available at URL: www.careleavers.com/research (accessed 26 June 2012)

Edwards, F. E. (1984) *Home or Away: Residential Child Care Strategy for the Eighties*, Glasgow: Strathclyde Regional Council

Eichsteller, G. (2009) 'The common third', *Children's webmag*. Available at URL: www.childrenwebmag.com/articles/social-pedagogy/some-basic-concepts-2-the-common-third (accessed 26 June 2012)

Eichsteller, G. and Holthoff, S. (2009) 'Risk competence: towards a pedagogic conceptualisation of risk', *Children's webmag*. Available at URL: www.childrenwebmag.com/articles/social-pedagogy/towards-a-pedagogic-conceptualisation-of-risk (accessed 26 June 2012)

Elsley, S. (2006) *No Time To Lose: A Manifesto for Children and Young People Looked After Away From Home*, Glasgow: Scottish Institute for Residential Child Care. Available at URL: www.celcis.org/resources/no_time_to_lose_a_manifesto_for_children_and_young_people_looked_after_away (accessed 18 July 2012)

Elsley, S. (2009) 'Who else has the magic wand? An evaluation of a residential unit for younger children', *Scottish Journal of Residential Child Care*, Vol. 8, No. 2, pp. 11–18. Available at URL: www.celcis.org/media/resources/publications/SJRCC81_magic_wand.pdf (accessed 17 July 2011)

Emond, R. (2004) 'Rethinking our understanding of the resident group in group care', *Child and Youth Care Forum*, Vol. 33, No. 3, pp. 193–207; doi: 10.1023/B:CCAR.0000029685.80364.7f

Forrester, D. (2008) 'Is the care system failing children?', *The Political Quarterly*, Vol. 79, No. 2, pp. 206–11; doi: 10.1111/j.1467-923X.2008.00927.x

Forrester, D., Goodman, K., Cocker, C., Binnie, C. and Jensch, G. (2009) 'What is the impact of public care on children's welfare? A review of research findings from England and Wales and their policy implications', *Journal of Social Policy*, Vol. 38, pp. 439–56; doi: 10.1017/s0047279409003110

Fulcher, L. (2001) 'Differential assessment of residential group care for children and young people', *British Journal of Social Work*, Vol. 31, No. 3, pp. 417–35; doi: 10.1093/bjsw/31.3.417

Fulcher, L. and Ainsworth, F. (eds). (2006) *Group Care Practice with Children and Young People Revisited*, New York: The Haworth Press

Fulcher, L. and Garfat, T. (2012) 'Outcomes that matter for children and young people in out-of-home care', *Reclaiming Children and Youth, Vol.* 20, No. 4, pp. 52–8

Gallagher, B., Brannan, C., Jones, R. and Westwood, S. (2004) 'Good practice in the education of children in residential care', *British Journal of Social Work*, Vol. 34, No. 8, pp. 1133–60; doi: 10.1093/bjsw/bch133

Gill, T. (2007) *No Fear: Growing up in a Risk Averse Society*, London: Calouste Gulbenkian Foundation. Available at URL: www.gulbenkian.org.uk/publications/publications/42-NO-FEAR.html (accessed 17 July 2012)

Gilligan, R. (2000) 'Adversity, resilience and young people: The protective value of positive school and spare time experiences', *Children and Society*, Vol. 14, pp. 37–41; doi: 10.1111/j.1099-0860.2000.tb00149.x

Gilligan, R. (2007) 'Spare time activities for young people in care: What can they contribute to educational progress?', *Adoption and Fostering*, Vol. 31, No. 1, pp. 92–9

Great Britain (1984) *Second Report from the Social Services Committee, Session 1983–84: Children in Care Vol.1 Report Together with the Proceedings of the Committee*. London: HMSO. Available at URL: https://catalogue.lse.ac.uk/Author/Home?author=Great%20Britain.%20Parliament.%20House%20of%20Commons.%20Social%20Services%20Committee (accessed 26 June 2012)

Great Britain (1987) *The Social Work (Residential Establishments-Child Care) (Scotland) Regulations 1987*, No. 2233 C.F.R. Section 150. Available at URL: www.legislation.gov.uk/uksi/1987/2233/contents/made (accessed 29 July 2012)

Hallett, C. (2000) 'Ahead of the game or behind the times? The Scottish children's hearings system in international context'. *International Journal of Law, Policy and the Family*, Vol. 14, No. 1, pp. 31–44; doi: 10.1093/lawfam/14.1.31

Hamalainen, J. (2003) 'The concept of social pedagogy in the field of social work', *Journal of Social Work*, Vol. 3, No. 1, pp. 60–80; doi: 10.1177/1468017303003001005

Happer, H., McCreadie, J. and Aldgate, J. (2006) *Celebrating success: What Helps Looked After Children Succeed*, Edinburgh: Social Work Inspection Agency.

Available at URL: www.scotland.gov.uk/Publications/2006/06/07121906/1 (accessed 26 June 2012)

Healthcare Policy and Strategy Directorate (2009) *Implementation of Action 15 of the Looked After Children and Young People: We Can and Must Do Better Report (CEL 16)*, Edinburgh: Scottish Government. Available at URL: www.sehd.scot.nhs.uk/mels/CEL2009_16.pdf (accessed 26 June 2012)

Hill, M. (2009) *Higher Aspirations, Brighter Futures: Matching Resources to Needs* report, NRCCI, Glasgow: Scottish Institute for Residential Child Care. Available at URL: www.celcis.org/media/resources/publications/F2.pdf (accessed 17 July 2012)

HMI/SWSI (2001) *Learning with Care: The Education of Children Looked After Away from Home by Local Authorities*. Edinburgh: Her Majesty's Inspectors of Schools and Social Work Services Inspectorate. Available at URL: www.educationscotland.gov.uk/inspectionandreview/Images/lwc_tcm4-712786.pdf (accessed 17 July 2012)

Holden, M. (2001) *Therapeutic Crisis Intervention*, New York: Cornell University Family Life Development Center, 5th edn

Howley, D. (2011) 'Foster carers cannot take the place of parents', *The Guardian*. Available at URL: www.guardian.co.uk/society/2011/jun/21/residential-care-home-children-fostering?INTCMP=ILCNETTXT3487 (accessed 26 June 2012)

HSE (2010) *Myth: Health and Safety Has Gone Mad!*, London: Health and Safety Executive. Available at URL: www.hse.gov.uk/myth/dec10.htm (accessed 26 June 2012)

Hughes, D. (2009) *Principles of Attachment-Focused Parenting: Effective Strategies to Care For Children*, New York: Norton

Jackson, S. and Cameron, C. (2010) *Young People from a Public Care Background: Establishing a Baseline of Attainment and Progression Beyond Compulsory Schooling in Five EU Countries*, London: Thomas Coram Research Unit, Institute of Education, University of London. Available at URL: http://tcru.ioe.ac.uk/yippee/Portals/1/Final%20Report%20of%20the%20YiPPEE%20Project%20-%20WP12%20Mar11.pdf (accessed 17 July 2012)

Jahnukainen, M. (2007) 'High-risk youth transitions to adulthood: A longitudinal view of youth leaving the residential education in Finland', *Children and Youth Services Review*, Vol. 29, No. 5, pp. 637–54; doi: 10.1016/j.childyouth.2007.01.009

Kendrick, A. (2010) *International Comparisons of Residential Child Care*. Edinburgh: Scottish Government. Available at URL: http://archive.scottish.parliament.uk/s3/committees/audit/inquiries/children%20in%20care/Suppevidence_ScottishGovernmentV1.pdf (accessed 26 June 2012)

Kent, R. (1997) *Children's Safeguards Review*, Edinburgh: Social Work Services Inspectorate for Scotland

LAAC Scottish Nurse Forum (2008) *Scottish LAAC and Throughcare Nurses: Resource Directory*. Available at URL: www.shcn.org.uk/docs/Oct08/LAAC_Nurse_Directory_2008.pdf (accessed 26 June 2012)

Lane, D. (1994) *An Independent Evaluation of the Residential Child Care Initiative*, London: CCETSW

Lerpiniere, J., Davidson, J., Hunter, L., Kendrick, A. and Anderson, M. (2007) *Residential Child Care 2007 Qualifications Audit*, Glasgow: SIRCC. Available at URL: www.celcis.org/resources/entry/residential_child_care_2007_qualifications_audit_2007 (accessed 17 July 2012)

Liddell, M., Donegan, T., Goddard, C. and Tucci, J. (2006) *The State of Child Protection: Australian Child Welfare and Child Development Developments 2005*, Melbourne: Australian Childhood Foundation. Available at URL: www.childhood.org.au/Assets/Files/6f88319e-90c7-4b8d-b208-cbea46913648.pdf (accessed 17 July 2012)

Maclean, K. and Gunion, M. (2003) 'Learning with care: The education of children looked after away from home by local authorities', *Adoption and Fostering*, Vol. 27, No. 2, pp. 20–31

Marshall, K., Jamieson, C. and Finlayson, A. (1999) *Edinburgh's Children: The Report of the Edinburgh Inquiry into Abuse and Protection of Children in Care*, Edinburgh: City of Edinburgh Council. Available at URL: www.scotland.gov.uk/About/kerelaw/publications/ed-child-rpt (accessed 17 July 2012)

McCracken, A. (1992) 'Residential schools after List D', in Lloyd, G. (ed.) (1992) *Chosen with Care? Responses to Disturbing and Disruptive Behaviour*, Edinburgh: Moray House Publications, pp. 110–17

McLaughlin, H. (2009) *Service-User Research in Health and Social Care*, London: Sage

McPheat, G., Milligan, I. and Hunter, L. (2007) 'What's the use of residential child care? Findings of two studies detailing current trends in the use of residential child care in Scotland', *Journal of Children's Services*, Vol. 2, No. 2, pp. 15–25; doi: 10.1108/17466660200700013

Meltzer, H., Lader, D., Corbin, T., Goodman, R. and Ford, T. (2004) *The Mental Health of Young People Looked After by Local Authorities in Scotland*. Edinburgh: The Stationery Office

Milligan, I. (2009) *Introducing Social Pedagogy into Scottish Residential Child Care: An Evaluation of the Sycamore Services Social Pedagogy Training Programme*, Glasgow: SIRCC. Available at URL: www.celcis.org/resources/introducing_social_pedagogy_into_scottish_residential_child_care_2009 (accessed 17 July 2012)

Milligan, I. (2010) 'F is for functions of residential care', in Burns, C., Feilberg, F. and Milligan, I. (eds) (2010) *A–Z of Residential Child Care,* Glasgow: SIRCC, pp. 18–20. Available at URL www.celcis.org/resources/a_z_of_residential_child_care_2010 (accessed 18 July 2012)

Milligan, I. (2011) 'Resisting risk-averse practice: The contribution of social pedagogy', *Children Australia*, Vol. 34, No. 4, pp. 207–13; doi: 10.1375/jcas.36.4.207

Milligan, I. and Furnivall, J. (2011) 'The Scottish children's home: An evolving model of residential provision for vulnerable children', *Children Australia*, Vol. 36, No. 2, pp. 66–73; doi: 10.1375/jcas.36.2.66

Milligan, I., Hunter, L. and Kendrick, A. (2006) *Current Trends in the Use of Residential Child Care in Scotland*, Glasgow: SIRCC. Available at URL: www.celcis.org/resources/current_trends_in_the_use_of_residential_child_care_in_scotland (accessed 18 July 2012)

Milligan, I. and Stevens, I. (2006) *Residential Child Care: Collaborative Practice*, London: Sage

Murphy, J. (1992) *British Social Services: The Scottish Dimension*, Edinburgh: Scottish Academic Press

NHS Education for Scotland (2008) *A Capability Framework for Nurses Who Care for Children and Young People Who Are Looked After Away From Home*. Edinburgh: NHS Education for Scotland. Available at URL: www.mnic.nes. scot.nhs.uk/media/17530/lac_framework_finalfinal.pdf (accessed 26 June 2012)

NISW (1998) *A Golden Opportunity: A Report on Training and Staff Development for People Working in Residential Services for Children and Young People*, London: National Institute for Social Work

Norrie, K. M. (1997) *Children's Hearings in Scotland*, Edinburgh: Green, 2nd edn

ODS Consulting (2011) *Commissioning Social Care Services: Focus Groups with Social Care Service Providers*, Edinburgh: Audit Scotland. Available at URL: www.audit-scotland.gov.uk/docs/health/2012/nr_120301_social_care.pdf (accessed 17 July 2012)

Paige, R. and Clark, G. A. (eds) (1977) *Who Cares? Young People in Care Speak Out*, London: National Children's Bureau.

Parton, N. (2006) *Safeguarding Childhood: Early Intervention and Surveillance in a Late Modern Society*, Basingstoke: Palgrave Macmillan

Paterson, S., Watson, D. and Whiteford, J. (2003) *Let's Face It!: Young People Tell Us How It Is*, Glasgow: Who Cares? Scotland

Perry, B. (2009) 'Examining child maltreatment through a neurodevelopmental lens: Clinical applications of the neurosequential model of therapeutics', *Journal of Loss and Trauma*, Vol. 14, No. 4, pp. 240–55; doi: 10.1080/15325020903004350

Petrie, P. J. B., Cameron, C. E. H., McQuail, S., Simon, A. and Wigfall, V. (2009) *Pedagogy – A Holistic, Personal Approach to Work with Children and Young People, Across Services*, London: TCRU. Available at URL: http://eprints.ioe. ac.uk/58/1/may_18_09_Ped_BRIEFING__PAPER_JB_PP_.pdf (accessed 17 July 2012)

Piper, H., Powell, J. and Smith, H. (2006) 'Parents, professionals and paranoia: The touching of children in a climate of fear', *Journal of Social Work*, Vol. 6, No. 2, pp. 151–67; doi: 10.1177/1468017306066742

Pösö, T., Kitinoja, M. and Kekoni, T. (2010) 'Locking up for the best interests of the child – some preliminary remarks on "special care"', *Youth Justice*, Vol. 10, No. 3, pp. 245–57; doi: 10.1177/1473225410381687

Punch, S., Dorrer, N., Emond, R. and McIntosh, I. (2009) *Food Practices in Residential Children's Homes: The Views and Experiences of Staff and Children*, Stirling: University of Stirling. Available at URL: www.ncb.org.uk/ media/518085/ncercc_stirling_food_staffhandbook.pdf (accessed 17 July 2012)

Residential Health Care Project Team (2004) *Forgotten Children: Addressing the Health Needs of Looked After Children and Young People*, Edinburgh: Astron

Riverside Sites (2008) 'Sons of the Mars'. Available at URL: www.sonsofthemars.

com (accessed 26 June 2012)

Scotland's Commissioner for Children and Young People (2008) *Sweet 16?: The Age of Leaving Care in Scotland*. Available at URL: www.sccyp.org.uk/webpages/Leaving_Care_Report_for_Web_20080325.pdf (accessed 12 May 2008)

Scottish Executive (2000) *The Same As You? A Review of Services for People With Learning Disabilities*, Edinburgh: Scottish Executive. Available at URL: www.scotland.gov.uk/Resource/Doc/1095/0001661.pdf (accessed 26 June 2012)

Scottish Executive (2002) *It's Everyone's Job To Make Sure I'm Alright: Report of the Child Protection Audit and Review*, Edinburgh: Scottish Executive. Available at URL: www.scotland.gov.uk/Publications/2002/11/15820/14009 (accessed 26 June 2012)

Scottish Executive (2005) *National Care Standards: Care Homes for Children and Young People*, Edinburgh: Scottish Executive. Available at URL: www.scotland.gov.uk/Publications/2011/05/16141058/9 (accessed 26 June 2012)

Scottish Executive (2007) *Looked After Children and Young People: We Can and Must Do Better*, Edinburgh: Scottish Executive. Available at URL: www.scotland.gov.uk/Publications/2007/01/15084446/0 (accessed 26 June 2012)

Scottish Government (2005) *National Care Standards: Care Homes for Children and Young People*, Edinburgh: Scottish Government. Available at URL: www.scotland.gov.uk/Publications/2011/05/16141058/0 (accessed 26 June 2012)

Scottish Government (2008a) *Getting It Right For Every Child: An Overview of the Getting It Right Approach*, Edinburgh: Scottish Government. Available at URL: www.scotland.gov.uk/gettingitright (accessed 26 June 2012)

Scottish Government (2008b) *These Are Our Bairns: A Guide for Community Planning Partnerships on Being a Good Corporate Parent*, Edinburgh: Scottish Government. Available at URL: www.scotland.gov.uk/Publications/2008/08/29115839/0 (accessed 26 June 2012)

Scottish Government (2009) *Securing Our Future Initiative: A Way Forward for Scotland's Secure Care Estate: A Response from the Scottish Government and COSLA*, Edinburgh: Scottish Government. Available at URL: www.scotland.gov.uk/Publications/2009/04/23163903/1 (accessed 26 June 2012)

Scottish Government (2011) *Educational Outcomes of Looked After Children 2009/10*, Edinburgh: Scottish Government. Available at URL: www.scotland.gov.uk/Publications/2011/06/23123831/0 (accessed 26 June 2012)

Scottish Government (2012a) *Children's Social Work Statistics Scotland*, Edinburgh: Scottish Government. Available at URL: www.scotland.gov.uk/Resource/0038/00388582.pdf (accessed 26 June 2012)

Scottish Government (2012b) *Children's Social Work Statistics Scotland, No. 1: 2012 edn*, Edinburgh: Scottish Government. Available at URL: www.scotland.gov.uk/Publications/2012/02/7586 (accessed 26 June 2012)

Scottish Office (1997) *The Children (Scotland) Act 1995, Regulations and Guidance, Vol 2: Children Looked After By Local Authorities*, Edinburgh: Scottish Office. Available at URL: www.scotland.gov.uk/Publications/2004/10/20067/44723 (accessed 26 June 2012)

Scottish Parliament (2012) *The Educational Attainment of Looked After Children*, Edinburgh: The Scottish Parliament. Available at URL: www.scottish.

parliament.uk/parliamentarybusiness/CurrentCommittees/51538.aspx (accessed 17 July 2012)

SCRA (2011a) *SCRA Annual Report 2010/11*. Stirling: Scottish Children's Reporter Administration. Available at URL: www.scra.gov.uk/cms_resources/Annual%20Report%201011.html (accessed 17 July 2012)

SCRA (2011b) *SCRA Statistical Analysis 2010/11*. Stirling: Scottish Children's Reporter Administration. Available at URL: www.scra.gov.uk/cms_resources/Statistical%20Analysis%202010-11.pdf (accessed 17 July 2012)

Sempik, J., Ward, H. and Darker, I. (2008) 'Emotional and behavioural difficulties of children and young people at entry to care', *Clinical Child Psychology and Psychiatry*, Vol. 13, No. 2, pp. 221–33; doi: 10.1177/1359104507088344

Shaw, T. (2007) *An Independent Review of the Systems in Place to Protect Children and Keep Them Safe in Residential Care Between 1950–1995*. Edinburgh: Scottish Government. Available at URL: www.scotland.gov.uk/Publications/2007/11/20104729/0 (accessed 26 June 2012)

Siebelt, L., Morrison, E. and Cruickshank, C. A. (2008) *Caring About Success: Young People's Stories*, Glasgow: Who Cares? Scotland

SIRCC (2006) *No Time to Lose: A Manifesto for Children Looked After Away From Home*, Glasgow: Scottish Institute for Residential Child Care. Available at URL: www.celcis.org/resources/entry/no_time_to_lose_a_manifesto_for_children_and_young_people_looked_after_away (accessed 17 July 2012)

SIRCC (2009) *Securing Our Future: A Way Forward for Scotland's Secure Care Estate*, Glasgow: Scottish Institute for Residential Child Care. Available at URL: www.celcis.org/resources/securing_our_future_a_way_forward_for_scotlands_secure_care_estate_2009 (accessed 18 July 2012)

SIRCC (2010a) *Go Outdoors! Guidance and Good Practice on Encouraging Outdoor Activities in Residential Child Care*, Glasgow: Scottish Institute for Residential Child Care. Available at URL: www.celcis.org/resources/go_outdoors_guidance_and_good_practice_on_encouraging_outdoor_activities_in (accessed 18 July 2012)

SIRCC (2010b) *Reflections + Visions: The World Through Different Eyes*. Glasgow: Scottish Institute for Residential Child Care. Available at URL: www.celcis.org/resources/reflections_visions_the_world (accessed 26 June 2012)

Skinner, A. (1992) *Another Kind of Home: A Review of Residential Child Care*. Edinburgh: Scottish Office

Smith, M. (2009) *Rethinking Residential Child Care: Positive Perspectives*, Bristol: The Policy Press

Smith, M. and Milligan, I. (2005) 'The expansion of secure accommodation in Scotland: In the best interests of the child?', *Youth Justice*, Vol. 4, No. 3, pp. 178–91; doi: 10.1177/147322540400400303

Stalker, K. (2008) 'Disabled children in residential settings', in Kendrick, A. (ed.) (2008) *Residential Child Care Prospects and Challenges*, London: Jessica Kingsley, pp. 107–20

Steckley, L. (2005) 'Just a game?: The therapeutic potential of football', in Crimmens, D. and Milligan, I. (eds), *Facing Forward: Residential Child Care in the 21st Century*, Lyme Regis: Russell House, pp. 137–48

Steckley, L. (2010) 'Containment and holding environments: Understanding and reducing physical restraint in residential child care', *Children and Youth Services Review*, Vol. 32, No. 1, pp. 120–8; doi: 10.10.1016/j. childyouth.2009.08.007

Stein, M. (2002) *Still A Bairn? A Study of Throughcare and Aftercare Services in Scotland*, Edinburgh: Scottish Executive. Available at URL: www.scotland. gov.uk/Publications/2002/06/14924/7628 (accessed 17 July 2012)

Stein, M. (2012) *Care Less Lives: The Story of the Rights Movement of Young People in Care*, London: Catch 22

SWIA (2005) *An Inspection into the Care and Protection of Children in Eilean Siar*. Edinburgh: Scottish Executive. Available at URL: www.scswis.com/ index.php?option=com_docman&task=doc_details&gid=197&Itemid=703 (accessed 17 July 2012)

SWIA (2009) *Guide to Strategic Commissioning: Taking a Closer Look at Strategic Commissioning in Social Work Services,* Edinburgh: Social Work Inspection Agency. Available at URL: www.scotland.gov.uk/Publications/2009/09/17112552/10 (accessed 26 June 2012)

SWSIS (1996) *A Secure Remedy: 114A Review of the Role, Availability and Quality of Secure Accommodation for Children in Scotland*, Edinburgh: Social Work Services Inspectorate for Scotland

SWSIS (1999) *The Report of the National Planning Group on Care and Education Services for Young People With Behavioural Problems, Including Offending*, Edinburgh: Social Work Services Inspectorate for Scotland

United Nations (1989) *United Nations Convention on the Rights of the Child*. Available at URL: www2.ohchr.org/english/bodies/crc (accessed 18 July 2012)

Utting, W. (1991) *Children in Public Care: A Review of Residential Care*, London: HMSO

Vrouwenfelder, E., Milligan, I. and Merrell, M. (2012) *Social Pedagogy and Inter-Professional Practice: Evaluation of Orkney Islands Training Programme*, Glasgow: Scottish Institute for Residential Child Care/Centre for Excellence in Looked After Children in Scotland. Available at URL: www.celcis.org/ resources/entry/social_pedagogy_and_inter_professional_practice_evaluation_of_orkney_island (accessed 17 July 2012)

Ward, A. (2007) *Working in Group Care: Social Work and Social Care in Residential and Day Care Settings*, Bristol: Policy Press

Warner, N. (1992) *Choosing With Care: The Report of the Committee of Enquiry into the Selection, Development and Management of Staff in Children's Homes*. London: HMSO

Watson, D. (2004) 'Let's face it!: Young people tell us how it is', *Scottish Journal of Residential Child Care*, Vol. 3, No. 1, pp. 47–59. Available at URL: www.celcis. org/media/resources/publications/lets_face_it.pdf (accessed 17 July 2012)

Watson, N. (2006) *Dundee: A Short History*, Edinburgh: Black and White

White, K. J. (2008) 'The ideology of residential care and fostering', *Children Webmag*. Available at URL: www.childrenwebmag.com/articles/foster-care/ the-ideology-of-residential-care-and-fostering (accessed 26 June 2012)

Wilson, A. (2009) 'Helping looked-after children and young people cope when they are ill'. *Scottish Journal of Residential Child Care*, Vol. 8, No. 2, pp. 33–40.

Available at URL: www.celcis.org/media/resources/publications/SJRCC82_
helping_ill_children.pdf (accessed 17 July 2012)

INDEX